Christianity Challenges the University

edited by
Peter Wilkes

InterVarsity Press
Downers Grove
Illinois 60515

InterVarsity Press is the book-publishing division of Inter-Varsity Christian Fellowship, a student movement active on campus at hundreds of universities, colleges and schools of nursing. For information about local and regional activities, write IVCF, 233 Langdon St., Madison, WI 53703.

Distributed in Canada through InterVarsity Press, 1875 Leslie St., Unit 10, Don Mills, Ontario M3B 2M5, Canada.

Biblical quotations, unless otherwise noted, are from the Revised Standard Version of the Bible, copyrighted 1946, 1952, © 1971, 1973, and are used by permission.

ISBN 0-87784-474-7

Printed in the United States of America

Library of Congress Cataloging in Publication Data
Main entry under title:

Christianity challenges the university.

"Lectures presented in the Great Hall of the Memorial Union at the University of Wisconsin, Madison"-Foreword.
Includes bibliographies.
Contents: The christian world view / Peter Wilkes-Man, naked ape and nothing more? / Wayne M. Becker-Christian doubts about economic dogmas / [etc.]
1. Christianity and culture-Addresses, essays, lectures. I. Wilkes, Peter, 1937-
BR115.C8C447   261.5   81-2268
ISBN 0-87784-474-7   AACR2

| 17 | 16 | 15 | 14 | 13 | 12 | 11 | 10 | 9 | 8 | 7 | 6 | 5 | 4 | 3 | 2 | 1 |
| 95 | 94 | 93 | 92 | 91 | 90 | 89 | 88 | 87 | 86 | 85 | 84 | 83 | 82 | 81 |

Contents

Foreword

This book is a written version of five lectures presented
in the Great Hall of the Memorial Union at the
University of Wisconsin, Madison. It bears the char-
acteristics of its birth process in that the lecture format
does not permit much excursion into detail. The
purpose of publication in book form is to encourage others
in universities to participate in such public discussions
and to illustrate how it was done on one prestigious
midwestern state campus.
The Publisher

Chapter 1
Introduction

Peter Wilkes

The American university is an enormously influential institution. To the top fifty or so academic establishments, government and industry have come cap in hand, a-wooing. As a result, American academia is deeply committed to an institutional marriage, with a dowry measured in millions if not billions of dollars. For major universities, that liaison has meant commitment on an unparalleled scale to research. Since the funding controls the direction the research must take, both knowledge itself (at least as measured by volume) and the university are influenced by society in general and by government in particular. In return the research-oriented university gains not only money for students and equipment but influence for its faculty. These major institutions provide an intellectual resource for all branches of government and industry. Planes leaving such places as Boston, Chicago, Oakland (near Berkeley) and Madison for Washington, D.C., are crowded with professors seeking not only funding but also influence. Professors witness to congressional committees, deliberate with administration officials and serve on committees in national administrative departments.

A second, less dramatic opportunity for influence is available to all universities simply because they are teaching institutions. Into their halls crowd young people destined by society to be its leaders in a multitude of areas. Because students will become leaders, equality of opportunity for racial and ethnic minorities as well as for women has become an educational issue. Minorities and women know very well that the path to the boardroom and to the president's office usually begins in the university classroom. It is part of the genius of America that its universities have been opened to a far wider range of its citizens than the older, elite-oriented institutions in Europe. Today's equal opportunity programs are the logical successors of our forebears' commitment to educate all who could benefit to as high a level as possible.

With that commitment, power and influence over an entire culture were handed to those who would teach these millions. During the years when many crucial decisions of their lives are being made, young potential leaders open their minds to their teachers. Students are influenced not only by what is said but also by unstated assumptions. Professors' attitudes to life, in their public activities as well as inside the lecture room, affect young people.

Universities have been conscious of that influence from the start. In medieval Europe the Roman Catholic Church struggled to control the scholars of the great universities—and failed. It was no accident that Martin Luther was a professor, or that the English Reformation began with John Wycliffe at Oxford. When Henry VIII and his supporters financed the universities heavily, they were seeking influence and control. But the heartening feature is that such attempts invariably fail. The people who hold the purse strings of universities have rarely managed to stifle criticism of themselves or their status. The religious suppression of yesterday failed. The political suppression attempted in so many parts of the world is also failing. Students are always in the vanguard of social change. The lecturers in this series are convinced that the more subtle efforts of secular suppression will also fail.

Attempts to mold university opinion fail because the academic community holds certain cultural values. Indeed, it is its essential function to safeguard the intellectual heritage against all comers. In medieval and Reformation times academics could see themselves maintaining the religious basis of truth using intellectual weapons. In the universities the "new knowledge" was seen as a means to recovering the truth from its political and superstitious accretions.

Since the eighteenth century, a profound shift in the whole idea of the role of the university has taken place. The idea of safeguarding a heritage has waned in influence and has been replaced by an intellectual defense of secular culture.

All cultures have their gods, and the god of secular culture is Man. In the secular culture of today's university every value becomes subordinated to that god. Culture itself is defended as worthwhile because it belongs to Man. The only knowledge that matters is knowledge that directly benefits or glorifies Man. The basis for morals is Man.

In spite of that, the idolatrous view of Man is rarely discussed in the university. It is imposed by implication. It is the intellectual bedrock on which much of science and the humanities rests. Students absorb it without discussion, appreciation or criticism because it is not mentioned. It is simply assumed.

The idolatry is therefore difficult to oppose. It is so pervasive that even when radicals seek to throw it down, they erect in its place a further image of the same lord.

A Christian professor in the modern secular university must oppose that secularized culture. The issue is basic to the Christian faith. Pride of Man is the essence of sin. It represents the unattainable desire for Man to be something over against God. A Christian intellectual is therefore necessarily committed to total war with secularism. There can be no comfortable compromise.

As we have noted, the stakes in this struggle are enormous. It is not merely a battle for the soul of the university; the prize is influence over the entire culture which is the heritage of the modern university. The Christian case is so fundamental a challenge to secular assumptions that it touches every sphere of human activity. The whole secular perspective for science and its use, for human values and ethics, for what people *are* and ought to be, is different from a Christian point of view. As the old optimistic view of Man manifests its bankruptcy, Christian professors have an opportunity for leverage on the whole society. In the name of the Lord Jesus they can use their expertise to remold their specialties to conformity with a Christian world view.

The task is of course enormous. As we have seen, one must stand against the trend of educated opinion since the eighteenth century. It is therefore not surprising that most Christian professors maintain their beliefs privately or perhaps in personal witness but keep quiet in their institutions. To do that, however, is to misunderstand the situation. Simply to continue to operate silently in the secular world is to support its contention that Man is God and that God is irrelevant. Each silent Christian professor confirms for the student multitude that the beliefs of secularism are unchallenged and unchallengeable.

Yet there has never been a better time to speak than the present. As many students of the twentieth century have noted, the secular humanist view of Man has led to disaster. Human beings turn out to have feet of clay. Human beings not only contemplate the heavens but also pollute the earth. Where once wars were fought for religion and trade, now they are fought for secular ideology: Marxist proletarian

Man versus capitalist Man.

In such a context Christians have a ready audience on campus. The old liberal humanism is tinged with disillusion and many are ready to listen to the Christian alternative, an alternative far more radical than the radicals can conceive.

One group of professors on the Madison, Wisconsin, campus who had been meeting regularly for prayer felt themselves called to make some sort of public statement. The possibility was approached somewhat nervously. After all, to get a name for religious enthusiasm is not likely to enhance one's academic career. But the imperatives of our situation were clear, and in the end we could do no other.

We selected a title for the series, assigned the subjects, booked the union Great Hall (in faith asking for 200 chairs) and sought the help of Christian students in distributing posters. Each week for five successive Monday lunchtimes we were overwhelmed with student response. The seating was totally inadequate and we had to more than double the number of chairs. The floor, windowsills and stairs held the overflow.

When it was all over we came to the conviction that what we had done could be done at any university. When a group of professors, including distinguished scholars, takes the opportunity to speak out in the university, others will listen. We acknowledge that the step was a small one, but it is our hope that by many such small steps the journey to the kingdom may be made.

Chapter 2
The Christian World View—
A Radical Alternative

Peter Wilkes

A world view is the intellectual framework by means of which we correlate all our experience in the world and make coherent sense out of it. That experience includes everything about the "external" world which comes to me via my senses and also those internal awarenesses I have about myself.

A world view is basic to every person's existence. By it we react to and operate on the world around us and establish for ourselves what we *are*. It is at once the foundation both for self-awareness and for action in the world.

The definition should make clear why we all *must* have at least one world view. It is simply not possible to operate in the world as a human being without *some* way of making sense out of experience. The difficulty, of course, is that we may have not just *one* world view but two or three or even more. At work I operate as a scientist striving for objectivity in my experiments. At home I may work on quite different logical bases as a husband, father, ball player, observer of

TV or any of the other things that even professors are known to indulge in.

The aim of the thoughtful individual since Socrates (and perhaps before that) is to operate with one world view capable of making sense out of *all* experience in a natural way. It will be our contention in this series that Christianity provides such a world view.

First, however, we need to look at a problem. Since a world view is a framework for understanding data, the data themselves cannot provide the framework. They may suggest an area in which a framework is needed, but they cannot substitute for it. Our world view, therefore, must be built from a set of presuppositions which we use without being able to prove. That is why we call them *presuppositions*. They are supposed prior to the data and are not obtained by reflection on our experience. *They* are the means by which we reflect.

If all that sounds complicated, permit me an example which illustrates what is really a simple point. We cannot help being aware of the external world through our eyes. But to understand our vision we have to analyze it in a three-dimensional frame. People who are born blind, and who later achieve sight as adults, have to learn that process, but it proves difficult for them to make sense of their impressions. The three-dimensional frame by which we interpret our binocular vision is distinct from the vision itself.

There is a further point in the illustration. We have no choice in the interpretation; it reflects the facts of our own construction. We are bound to the presupposition of three-dimensionality.

We conclude that at least some of our presuppositions are forced on us by our natures and that we have no logical system for testing them in advance. Instead they provide the axioms for our logic. All the logic can do is to test whether the presuppositions are compatible with each other.

This important limit on the proper use of logical argument may be unpalatable, but is nonetheless real.

Intellectual Honesty and the University

Now let me answer another question. Why should a group of five diverse professors be so concerned with the issue of Christianity and secular dogmas that we find ourselves addressing a large throng of students in this series? Believe me, it would be much easier and less intimidating to proceed quietly with my research in the engineering college.

We are giving these lectures because we sense that within the university it has become established practice to operate from a world view without ever saying what it is. Since some of the world views used in formal lectures are antithetical to Christianity we want to draw attention to what is happening.

We believe that if professors start from a Marxist position in an area like political philosophy or sociology they should say so frankly. The results that flow from such a position will then be seen by students to be a consequence of that stance. I believe we owe it to the honesty of our intellectual discipline and to our students to make it clear that our lectures are not "received truth" handed down from professional heights but deductions from experience based on our world view.

If the university is to practice that "fearless sifting and winnowing" which is the basis for its existence as a "marketplace for ideas" a deeper level of honesty is demanded. We Christians are here trying to articulate our position in the hope that others will respond. We can then debate about the deeper issues on which our lives are based, but which are often ignored or confused in the secular world of the university.

Since that sounds like a tall order, a note of limitation may be appropriate. In defending a Christian world view we are doing that and no more. We are emphatically *not* defending that vast history of abuses of the Christian world view which have occurred in the past. It is after all perfectly possible to discuss the merits of Marxism without defending its malpractice in Soviet Russia. Similarly, we can sensibly defend Christianity without having to defend an appalling list of terrible mistakes carried out in its name but in flagrant abuse of its principles.

God and the World
A Christian world view begins with God. We are people of the book which begins, "In the beginning God. . . ." God exists outside nature and outside humanity and quite independent of both. Unbelieving critics have rarely understood how profound and far-reaching that is, as we shall see.

Note that God's existence is not a postulate to be proved by logical argument, as has so often been attempted in the past. If I can carry out an analysis about whether or not God exists, I am automatically assuming that I have a fundamental framework within which I can place God in order to work out God's relation to other things. It is precisely this that I am *not* saying about God.

On the contrary, my contention is that the existence of God is the foundation for the Christian world view, a presupposition, a basis on which the rest of the system is to be built.

It follows that the famous "proofs" of God are not merely wrong in logic (although I suspect they are), but in addition are wrong in conception. They should never be attempted. In them God becomes secondary, contingent on us, whereas the Christian position is that we are dependent in every sense on him.

A second feature of the Christian world view follows naturally. The world is created by God and humankind is part of nature. From such an obvious statement the conclusions are surprisingly important.

First, nature matters. It is to be taken seriously. It is no accident that modern experimental science developed in Christian Europe. It did so because Christianity takes the real world seriously. It does not treat it as myth or illusion as some of the eastern religions do. Rather it demands that actions in the world be treated responsibly and seriously.

Second, the statement provides an explanation for the extraordinary fact that the world appears to us as rational. That assumption lies at the heart of science. Albert Einstein, perhaps the greatest modern scientist, commented, "To understand why nature is thus and not otherwise, is for the scientific mind, the highest satisfaction; that if I may say so is the religious basis for scientific effort." Whitehead, the philosopher of science, makes the same point: "Faith in reason is the trust that the ultimate nature of things lie together in a harmony which excludes mere arbitrariness. It is the faith that at the basis of things we shall not find mere arbitrary mystery."

The world corresponds to thought because both humankind and the world are created by a rational being, whom we call God. Science is, therefore, explicable within the context of a Christian position.

The study of nature includes the study of human beings. In biology, psychology and sociology the scientific approach has had considerable success. Since human beings are part of the world, in the Christian view it is appropriate to study humankind as human animal, and success is to be expected and indeed encouraged. Professor Becker in the following lecture will explore the limitation of such a view, since the Christian position is that while *homo sapiens* is indeed an animal as part of the world, that is not all he or she is. Professor Richardson will illustrate the problems that arise when human beings are viewed as merely part of an economic system. In all these cases our view is that there is *more* to being human.

Humanity and Christianity
The third point in the Christian world view is the basis for
the idea that humanity is "something more." The view that
man is somehow different is pervasive. We have great difficulty denying it in practice even though it is often denied
in principle. When we do that, the confusion that then
arises can be instructive.

Christians regard humankind as operating on three
levels. First, each individual operates as a subject regarding
the world as object. That is what science is all about. Its essence lies in the detached observer trying to understand
without being involved.

Second, humankind also exists within a network of
subject-subject relations. In the world of human relations
a human being operates sometimes as subject and sometimes as object. Or we are both subject and object simultaneously. At this level even when we act "objectively" upon
other humans we cannot help being influenced by the fact
that they *are* human. Thus our actions include some degree
of consciousness of what the other is feeling.

It is precisely our ability to react that way which makes up
our humanness. To be otherwise is to become "inhuman."
Loving one another obviously requires such an exchange.
Morals and ethics are built on it also. This is the actual business of living and dying as a human being.

At this level to try to operate scientifically as a detached
experimentalist is ridiculous and inappropriate. It is to
cease to be human and to attempt the impossible. The difference between functioning in the subject-object realm of
science and the subject-subject realm of human relations is
easy to illustrate. In those splendid English double-decker
buses, large notices forbid the traveling populace from spit-
ting. A visiting scientist might be intrigued that such notices
are made of anodized aluminum, or exhibit a certain sym-
metry of the letters. Yet the ordinary Englishman concludes that if he expectorates, he will be liable to a $50 fine!

The objective scientific analyses may be correct, but there is a meaning to which they do not penetrate. On reading the notice, one finds himself addressed; the reader is in a subjective situation, receiving a message and obliged to react. He is immediately in the world of interpersonal relations.

If we stand back and observe other humans as things we can try to be objective. People then appear at one with the animal kingdom and the answers obtained are consistent with those assumptions. To study people at the subject-subject level, however, is to be engaged. The questions we then ask and the answers we obtain are quite different. Secular humanism has never been able to provide a world view that encompasses both. Christianity does so by recognizing a third and higher level for human existence which alone makes sense of the other two.

At that third level, the object-subject level, each person finds himself or herself to be the object being acted on by God. As at the second level, human beings are addressed, and detached observation is inappropriate. Instead we find ourselves called on to respond. The response is not to an equal, however, but to the Creator, to the Lord.

To the Christian, men and women bear the imprint of being designed for these three levels or modes of existence. That is what is meant by our creation "in the image of God" (Gen. 1:27). It implies that humans have the capacity to hear and respond to God. Immediately it is clear that the meaning of being human lies outside ourselves. We are only one end, the minor end, of a "conversation." To understand human nature we need to see something of the other end of the communication channel.

From this basic set of ideas about man, nature and God, the Christian is in a strong position to understand and explain human activity in a simple and straightforward way.

We can begin by noting that meaning and purpose in human existence can never be found by a scientific study. The conclusions we reach by that approach are limited by the framework within which the questions are asked. Questions of meaning, purpose and value cannot even be expressed in a scientific framework, let alone answered.

Suppose it is springtime and you have received a grant from the National Science Foundation to study young love. You scour the campus to find an eager young lover. You sit him down and strap onto him an assortment of hardware to measure his physical and mental responses. You then conduct an experiment by introducing his beloved into the laboratory and busily record his salivation, skin pigment, general agitation and accelerated pulse rate. When you have finished, you may have a scientific description of a set of responses to a stimulus but you have not even begun to understand what it is to be in love. To do that you have to approach the question in a different way, perhaps by abandoning your objectivity and experiencing it for yourself.

In our society there is a continual tendency to confuse the first two levels. Such confusion is evidence of the inadequacy of a purely materialistic world view. Behaviorists who explain human beings as entirely animal still go outside their laboratories and fall in love, and when they do, materialism is abandoned and an older world view takes over.

In contrast, our Christian world view finds its source of such ideals as love and justice in the upper object-subject level of human experience—in God himself. Within that framework no sophisticated sleight of hand is needed. The recognition of meaning and purpose in human life is personal. Spiritual relationships fit naturally alongside physical and material aspects of human life in the world.

The very objectivity of science which has made it so effective in the natural world is precisely the limitation which forever excludes it from the whole realm of personal relations. Yet for most of us that is the area that really matters.

It is very important that science is not excluded by an

artificial regulation. Christians are not on the battlements defending some sacred area from materialist hordes. It is rather that science by its *intrinsic* assumptions excludes itself from asking questions about values. Exactly the same subject may be studied, but the level of questioning differs. To return to our young lover—the meaning of his love simply cannot be addressed by a scientific approach, although certain aspects of his behavior can be.

Naturally, if you use one approach and exclude all others, you have predetermined the answers you will obtain. You may even conclude that love does not exist; there is nothing but a physical reaction. Such a conclusion is *not* scientific. It is a consequence of your world view which denies the possibility of asking subjective questions. Yet if you remain human you cannot avoid them, so you meet the bankruptcy of a materialistic world view face to face.

Protagoras once said, "Man is the measure of all things." On the contrary, the Christian replies, man is not even the measure of himself, for his meaning is inexorably fixed beyond his horizon. It lies in God alone.

It should by now be clear that if we cannot study men and women on certain levels scientifically, the same is true of God. I am reminded of the Soviet announcement after their first space flight, that they had been out into space to find God and lo! he was not there! I sometimes wonder if at the back of the spacecraft they had an inflatable cage in which they intended to entrap him and bring him back to earth as evidence of the victory of dialectical materialism.

Theirs was a peculiarly crass example of a frequent mistake. It was an attempt to take an objective position over against God, to make God object to our subject. Secular philosophers have always attempted that, yet the attempt is doomed to failure from the start. It is a misconception of both God and man.

Try to envision the possibility of Hamlet studying Shakespeare. The absurdity is at once evident. To us who exist

on the same level of reality as Shakespeare, however, every
act of Hamlet reveals the richness of his creator's mind.
In a somewhat similar way, the reality of human life is contingent on the more basic reality of God's existence.

The Search for Meaning

If as Christians we are right in our view that the value and
meaning that our natures demand have a source outside
ourselves, then a further question presses upon us. How
are we to find value and meaning if the objective approach
is excluded?

Even to phrase the question in that way is to begin to slide
into the objectivity trap. The truth is that we cannot help
finding and using our source of values all the time.

When we first began to experience the external world,
we did not have to seek it out. We knew it was there because
ever since we began splashing our breakfast cereal in our
eyes it has been pressing itself upon us. It is an awareness
intrinsic to our being.

Of course, in describing experience in this way I exclude
the more esoteric philosophers who are unsatisfied with
anything except a totally circular logical argument. They
sit contemplating their own navels in frozen inactivity as a
consequence.

An appropriate illustration of the importance of the
direct perception of values is the question of freedom. The
concept of freedom is notoriously slippery. My definition
of it is simply the internal awareness I have of an ability to
make a choice between options. Much of our life presupposes that such ability is common to us all. Our concept of
law is built on it. For example, if I am accused of an illegal
act and can demonstrate that I was forced to act by some-
body else, that is an acceptable defense: the act was *invol-
untary*.

In science itself as a human activity it is assumed that the
scientist can evaluate experimental results, *choose* rationally

between them and *decide* on new experiments. Our every-day speech and behavior are so full of the concept of an individual's freedom to choose that it seems impossible for us to live without it.

Nevertheless, to explain it remains a very knotty philosophical problem which no one seems able to solve to anybody else's satisfaction.

The characteristic secular approach is to try to find the source of our freedom by an objective "scientific" study, as we have already seen. If we objectively study man as an animal, then since the object becomes a *thing*, we are not surprised that he or she appears to be fully determined. Naturally, our internal awareness is irrelevant to the picture. Since that awareness is intrinsic to the practice of science, however, it is logically prior—which makes our deterministic conclusion invalid.

B. F. Skinner provides a delightful illustration of all this in his popular book *Beyond Freedom and Dignity*. After telling us that scientific study demonstrates that our freedom is an illusion and that we act only in conditioned responses, he leaps to the subjective level and proposes that we should *control* humanity by a rational *choice* of conditioning. (The words, *control* and *choice* of course, presuppose exactly the freedom he has denied to us.) In fact the very act of writing a book to persuade us that he is correct presupposes our ability to decide. The confusion has become hopeless. We are easily bemused by the sound of scientific argument into thinking that it has a wider validity than it does. So-called scientific humanism has made a fetish of that kind of confusion. It occurs each time the conclusions of objective study are applied to human beings as if they (or we) are *merely* animals and nothing more. Any world view in which it is proclaimed that its values are those of "scientific materialism" is caught in this confusion.

The confusion can be dangerous. C. S. Lewis noted that such use of objective thought is always applied to the rest of us by some "in-group." "The power of man to make himself what he pleases means the power of some men to make other men what they please." Skinner's response to that observation is devastating in its frankness. He simply says, "This is inevitable in the nature of cultural evolution." So much the worse for cultural evolution!

Hidden beneath all this confusion we can detect the essential problem for the humanist world view. Built into our very existence is a framework of values which includes freedom and some kind of moral sense (which is its corollary) without which we are incapable of making sense of our own existence. The humanist world view also depends on these values but has no explanation whatever for their existence. Any attempt to obtain them by observation of human beings results in a circular argument since the same values are used in the process.

Morals at the Subject-Subject Level
Because the existence of values is *experienced* at the interpersonal or subject-subject level, it is common to suppose that values are *obtained* there. So the next question is this: Can the values essential to a rational world view be obtained from humanity itself?

There are two obvious problems with the morals and meaning obtained that way. The first is that the morals used by people in various societies differ. If we could all examine ourselves and produce a statement of the inner moral compulsions which move us and they all turned out to be the same, we would have arrived experimentally at a universal moral. It is, however, abundantly clear that such is *not* the situation. The note of anguish in humanist manifestos is there precisely for that reason. Human affairs remain stubborn, pleas for harmony fall on deaf ears, ideology continues to divide us. There is experimentally no universal morality (but of course, if there were, Christians would ask why and would take it as a pointer to God).

The second problem in trying to obtain moral values and meaning from humanity itself is failure to satisfy the demand of universality. Secular humanists have long recognized that truth. Marx and Engels, for example, insist on it! "Justice," writes Engels, "is just the idealized glorified expression of existing economic relations." Marx comments, "Such phrases as 'a fair distribution' are obsolete verbal rubbish." Engels sneers, "How superstitious of LaSalle [the French socialist] to still believe in justice."

Marx and Engels, in their rigorous historical analysis of humanity, excluded moral values, seeing them as the fruits of class exploitation. Such a critique is always possible of man-generated morals and meaning.

In spite of that, Marx experienced the categorical imperative of an absolute moral. His great work, *Capital,* continually resorts to the violent language of moral outrage in his merciless exposure of the exploitation of the working-class poor of nineteenth-century England. Much of the attraction of Marxism has always lain in its high moral tone. In quoting the French socialist Louis Blanc in the Communist Manifesto, "from each according to his ability, to each according to his need," Marx was drawing on a sense of *universal* justice. Marxists have often followed their founder in thus rising above the restrictions of their own dialectic and expressing their humanness in moral demands. That is to their credit, but it exposes the impossibility in practice of avoiding moral commitment. Just as we cannot avoid operating on the basis of freedom (even when we deny its possibility), so we cannot help assuming the existence of an absolute morality.

The dangers of tyranny implicit in behaviorism are to be found also in the intellectual rejection of absolute moral values. Lenin added to the Marxist-Leninist doctrine that the proletariat would rule over the bourgeoisie with a rule "enforced by violence and unrestricted by law." Beyond Marx lay Lenin and beyond Lenin, the tyrant Stalin!

The Christian Basis for Morals

In contrast with the confusion implicit in all attempts to obtain morals and meaning at the person-person level, the Christian world view presents an elegant simplicity. Our sense of a universal moral imperative, an obligation to do the right, is reflection of our Creator in our created personalities.

The *ultimate* source of goodness and justice in the universe is God. Our experience of those values points up the creaturely nature of humanity which I have described as the object-subject relation.

Even so, confusion arises because humanity is flawed and the reflection of God is distorted. We are familiar with the term original sin. It is a fact that we human beings continually try to deny our creatureliness, our state of dependence on God. In our attempt to make Man an independent source of values we end up turning him (or her) into God. That is precisely what we mean by sin.

Our attempt at autonomy is inevitably self-defeating. We cannot deny our own natures even when we try, as we have seen. The confusion of secular dogmas is itself evidence of that impossibility. The essential nature of sin is reaching for the unattainable. Is it any wonder that secular man is confused?

Man's stubborn attempt at autonomy has many consequences. Among them are physical consequences, which Dr. MacKinney will address in his lecture.

Revelation

The highest level of our human nature implies the possibility of communication. Although we are objects to God's all-encompassing subjectivity, he insists on treating us with dignity as people and not as things. That is why we experience the inward call to goodness, justice and love.

That inward experience, however, is insufficient to overcome the confusion inherent in our flawed state. Indeed it leads all too easily to self-righteousness, to sin clothing itself in white robes. That tendency, at its worst when it is religious, demonstrates our ability to snatch defeat from the jaws of victory!

To human confusion and sinfulness God responds with revelation: objective, concrete revelation in time. God is not hidden, nor is his nature a matter of opinion. He revealed his goodness in the moral revelation to Moses and Israel recorded in the Old Testament. Revelation reached its height in Jesus, who claimed to be a living revelation of God's nature: "He who has seen me has seen the Father" (Jn. 14:9).

A claim to historical revelation requires, I think, some justification. First, to be effective it needs to be transmitted accurately. In my estimation the last century and a half of unremitting critical examination has led again and again to justification of the historical accuracy of the biblical record, as even a liberal critic like John A. T. Robinson has agreed. Professor Schoville will take up that point in his lecture.

A second requirement for revelation is that it should prove itself in some way. The miracles of Jesus were there expressly to authenticate his claims. That is particularly true of the resurrection. Jesus claimed that his death was to be God's method of dealing with human alienation from himself. His resurrection was the triumphant vindication of that claim. It was a demonstration that the human rebellion against God and its dark consequence of death had both been defeated.

The five professors participating in this series are themselves witnesses to the life-giving power of that message. We have found that the revelation of Jesus has the power to change our lives. The record of men and women who have found the Christian world view the only one to do justice to all our experience is truly impressive. It contains some of the greatest names in philosophy, the sciences, the arts and the humanities and it includes too, an innumerable multitude of ordinary people whose testimony continues to authenticate that revelation today.

A Radical Alternative

Why is Christianity a *radical* alternative? Radical means that it goes to the *root*. Christianity is pertinent to our desperate situation because it speaks to the problem at its root—the human heart. I have been reading feverishly in the last few weeks to prepare for this lecture, a whole sequence of books by humanists, scientists, secularists and materialists, all claiming to have the true world view. Among them I read *Chance and Necessity* by Jacques Monod. I was struck by the fact that after several hundred pages of proving that the objective path of studying man leads to the conclusion that there is no purpose, no meaning, no morals and quite possibly no future, Monod stops at the edge of the pit of despair. In the last three pages he cries out that somehow we *have* to find some kind of effective moral system. I honor the appeal that Monod makes because it is a human appeal, reaching out from heart to heart. I long to be able to tell him of the Christian world view, which I think can provide a sound basis for answering his questions, as I have tried to show.

The Christian world view is a basis for action. It provides a basis for the rule of law because it is realistic. It doesn't have a naive and optimistic view of human beings. It enables us to regard ourselves with a clear-eyed realism which takes into account the wars, the holocaust and all the other miseries that our own century has produced. We can see that human beings (including ourselves) are capable of falling into terrible traps. Indeed, we are often most dangerous when we are being most religious. Christians see all those things clearly and see the dangers. They know that checks and balances have to be built into any system because of the dangerous thing that man now is because of his flawed nature. Over and above that, Christians insist that people should behave the way they are created to behave, and we see in the gospel a basis for personal transformation that will satisfy that demand. It was an Old Testament prophet who wrote, "Let justice roll down like waters, and righteousness like an everflowing stream" (Amos 5:24). That must be the insistent cry of every Christian in every age. Wherever injustice rears its head there must be Christian people objecting to it and standing alongside those who suffer. Not to do that is to defy the whole basis of the world view that I've been trying to describe. Because in Christ God took on human suffering, his people can do no less if we really believe we are his people.

The action that results from this world view is radical because it is individual. The experience of radical Christianity always begins with a transformation of an individual life. We need not wait for the crowds to find the truth; we can experience it for ourselves. Once experienced, it becomes the basis for community and fellowship. But it starts with each one of us alone before God.

No longer the masses, the classes, the great groups that have so dominated the ideologies of the twentieth century, but the individual acting alone if necessary—that is the radical basis for continuing revolution. Because, of course, the problem is within. Bertrand Russell in one of his quieter moments wrote, "Love your enemies is good advice, but too difficult for us." Of course. It is precisely there that Christianity begins with the statement that men and women need the help of God. Finding God's help through Jesus Christ, we can overcome our sinfulness and can indeed love our enemies.

In Christ we confront the impossibility of the human situation, the pit of despair, with a love that is divine. Christ's love takes on death itself out of love for humankind. Christ's resurrection destroys the finality of death and through a new birth opens the way to a new life.

Recommended Reading

Barcus, Nancy. *Developing a Christian Mind.* Downers Grove: Inter-
  Varsity Press, 1977.
Blamires, Harry. *The Christian Mind.* Ann Arbor: Servant Books,
  1968.
Holmes, Arthur. *All Truth Is God's Truth.* Grand Rapids: Eerdmans,
  1977.
McKay, Donald. *Clockwork Image.* Downers Grove: InterVarsity
  Press, 1974.
Schaeffer, Francis A. *The God Who Is There.* Downers Grove: Inter-
  Varsity Press, 1968.
_____. *Escape from Reason.* Downers Grove: Inter-
  Varsity Press, 1968.
Sire, James W. *The Universe Next Door.* Downers Grove: InterVarsity
  Press, 1976.

Chapter 3
Man: Naked Ape and Nothing More?

Wayne M. Becker

A lecture series like this provides me with one of those rare opportunities to draw together into the same forum two topics that are exceedingly important to me—my academic profession and my religious faith. I come to campus every day with two hats, one labeled "biologist" and the other labeled "Christian." Usually I'm obliged to wear them one at a time, but this lecture gives me a chance to wear both of them at once. I am grateful for that, because I regard it as tremendously exciting to be a biologist, but am also aware that biology is the study of life with a small *l*. I see a lecture like this as an appropriate occasion to underscore my conviction that there is also a dimension of life that is meant to be spelled with a capital *L*. So I propose to wear both hats at once right now, seeking to share with you the difference it makes to look at life through the eyes of the "Christian alternative."

We ought to begin, I think, by asking—the Christian alternative to *what*? If it is our intention in this series to ad-

dress ourselves to the Christian alternative to secular dogmas, then clearly our starting point must in each case be a
long, hard look at the prevailing secular dogma to which we
are claiming an alternative—to which, indeed, we are claiming a *superior* alternative. In biology as perhaps in every
discipline, we come quickly to the heart of the matter when
we ask, what does secular wisdom have to say about the nature of man? You see, it is as we consider the nature and
meaning of man that the contrasts between secular thinking and the Christian alternative often come into sharpest
relief. That brings me to the title for this lecture, which
asks, poignantly I hope, "Man: Naked Ape and Nothing
More?"

The title of course derives from a very engaging book by
Desmond Morris called *The Naked Ape*,[1] first published in
1967 and now billed rather immodestly by the publisher as
"the sensational worldwide bestseller," which indeed it may
be. Morris is both an insightful zoologist and a gifted writer.
He describes the human animal as the naked ape that he in
reality is, mincing no words and stressing our intimate biological kinship with the animal kingdom. Morris explains
his emphasis well in his introduction, from which I quote:

> I am a zoologist and the naked ape is an animal. He is
> therefore fair game for my pen and I refuse to avoid him
> any longer simply because some of his behaviour pat-
> terns are rather complex and impressive. My excuse is
> that, in becoming so erudite, *Homo sapiens* has remained
> a naked ape nevertheless; in acquiring lofty new motives,
> he has lost none of the earthy old ones. This is frequently
> a cause of some embarrassment to him, but his old im-
> pulses have been with him for millions of years, his new
> ones only a few thousand at most—there is no hope of
> quickly shrugging off the accumulated genetic legacy of
> his whole evolutionary past. He would be a far less wor-
> ried and more fulfilled animal if only he would face up to
> this fact. Perhaps this is where the zoologist can help.[2]

I don't want to detract from Morris's efforts. I happen not to agree with all his inferences and conclusions, but I applaud his effort. He provides a perspective that we need, a reminder that, despite all our pretensions to the contrary, we as a species are intimately linked with the animal kingdom. We are, biologically speaking, an integral part of it.

This might be a good point at which to address a few words to some of my Christian friends who seem often to take strong exception to our kinship with the animal kingdom in general and with other primates in particular. As a biologist, I have trouble understanding that aversion. I wonder whether those who harbor it have ever stopped to consider how utterly our understanding of human physiology and our practice of medicine, for example, depend on exactly the kind of biological similarities between the human species and other animals that some seek to ignore or minimize. I am profoundly appreciative of the similarities. I applaud the basic unity of design and function that underlies all of biology. I am glad that the genetic code is universal, so that which is learned about bacteria often has relevance to human beings. I am glad that horse insulin corrects human diabetes. I am glad that my metabolism is so much like that of the rat and my vitamin requirements so similar to those of the guinea pig. We ought to have a litany of praise for our relatedness to the animal kingdom. It is the link that makes biomedical research on rats, guinea pigs and monkeys relevant to human health and well-being.

The Secular Dogma

The problem as I perceive it is not that Desmond Morris— or anyone else, for that matter—seeks to stress man's links with the rest of the animal kingdom or even to view man as a naked ape. The problem comes with a secular philosophy that is not satisfied simply to describe man as a naked ape, but insists on adding, *and nothing more:* a naked ape, and nothing more. The problem comes when science is used not just to describe and define man, but to circumscribe and limit man—to say that when the scientific description is complete, man stands fully defined and fully explained.

Having read Morris's book from cover to cover and taken note of all he has to say about such naked-ape activities as feeding, sleeping, fighting, grooming and mating, I find myself haunted by the question, "Is that all there is? Is all of reality to be found in the naturalist's notes? Are we really just naked apes and nothing more?"

If you turn to the chemist, things if anything get grimmer. The chemist painstakingly examines and analyzes the human body, reducing it to its constituent elements and compounds. A price is then assigned to each, the numbers are added up, and the claim is made that, at current market prices, the human body is worth a grand total of 97 cents. Let's go back to zoology! There at least we were naked apes.

But wait a moment. If you don't like the chemist's prices, the biochemist turns out to be more helpful. Writing recently in the *New York Times,* Prof. H. J. Morowitz of Yale University provided his own intriguing insights. Upset at the chemist's price tag of 97 cents, he wrote,

> I decided to make a thorough study of the entire matter. I started by sitting down with a catalogue from a biochemical company and began to list the ingredients. Hemoglobin was $2.95 a gram, purified trypsin was $36 a gram, and crystalline insulin was $47.50 a gram. I began to look at slightly less common constituents such as acetate kinase at $8,860 a gram. The real shocker came when I got to follicle-stimulating hormone at $4,800,000 a gram, clearly outside the reach of anything that Tiffany's could offer. For the really wealthy there is prolactin at $17,500,000 a gram, street price. Not content with a brief glance at the catalogue, I averaged all the constituents over the best estimate of their percentage in the composition of the human body and arrived at

$254.54 as the average price of a gram dry weight of human being. . . . The next computation was done with a great sense of excitement. I had to multiply the price per gram by my dry weight. The number literally jumped out at me—$6,000,015.44. I was a Six Million Dollar Man![3] Morowitz then went on to point out that the discrepancy between the 97-cent figure and the six-million-dollar price tag lies in the complexity of the molecules. He ended by noting that "we are, at the molecular level, the most information-dense structures around, surpassing by many orders of magnitude the best that computer engineers can design or even contemplate.

My point, however, is that all of this is just symptomatic, in a sense, of a secular world view that places inordinate confidence in our ability to understand and describe man in the same way and on the same terms as we seek to define and understand other phenomena in the natural world. Secular dogma insists that man is part of the natural world and can be fully understood as such. It is based on the presupposition that the only realities in the universe are those that can be explained and described in scientific terms, and that any assumptions to the contrary are not only unnecessary but invalid. Specifically, of course, it excludes the notion of God. As part of such a universe, man can be adequately and fully defined and delineated in terms of things that can be observed, measured and quantified. And in that outlook, when all the observations, measurements and quantitations are complete, our understanding of man will be complete. There is no value, purpose or meaning that lies beyond.

Such presuppositions are very significant. It is crucial that we recognize them as such—both because of the consequences that seem to flow logically from them, and also because of the contrast they afford to the presuppositions that underlie the Christian alternative. For the present, though, let's pursue this secular view a bit and see where it leads. In particular, I'd like to explore what it has to say about the past, where we've come from, and about the future, where we're going to. It seems to me that ultimately the values by which we live in the present are shaped by our conception of the past and our view of the future.

First, the past. Where do we come from, and what is the destiny that has already shaped our ends? For the answer of secular science, I turn to Dr. Jacques Monod, French molecular biologist and Nobel laureate, who presents the case eloquently in his recent book, *Chance and Necessity*.[4] The answer Monod espouses, of course, is evolution: "chance" in his title refers to random, unpredictable mutations; "necessity" refers to natural or Darwinian selection.

I want to make clear at this point that I have no quarrel with evolutionary theory per se. It seems to me a quite tenable hypothesis which accords well with much of the available scientific evidence. I find myself comfortable with evolution as theory, though I object when it is treated or presented as established fact. I am in fact reluctant to be drawn into controversies over creation *versus* evolution, preferring rather to think of creation *by* evolution. I will come back to that idea later. For the moment, suffice it to say that I have no particular objection to the evolutionary viewpoint. My quarrel lies rather with the philosophical framework in which it is usually understood and presented, a framework that is especially visible in Monod's writings.

His argument in *Chance and Necessity* is sophisticated and relies on data and judgment concerning molecular and cellular structure. Nonetheless, the primary thrust of his book is not scientific but philosophic. Much of what he says is based not so much on his scientific investigations as on his philosophic presuppositions. Listen to the way Monod puts it:

Chance alone is at the source of every innovation, of all creation in the biosphere. Pure chance, absolutely free but blind, at the very root of the stupendous edifice of evolution. This central concept of modern biology is no longer one among other possible or even conceivable hypotheses. It is today the sole conceivable hypothesis. And nothing warrants the supposition—or the hope—that on this score our position is likely ever to be revised.[5]

The Consequences

That kind of argument becomes for Monod, and for many scientists like him, the basis of their entire view of reality. They assume that the only thinkable position is that man is "the result of the impersonal plus time plus chance," as Francis Schaeffer puts it.[6] With such a position, there is nothing in the universe to which man can appeal with regard to purpose or values. Man, whoever or whatever he is, is alone. Near the end of his book, Monod writes, "If he accepts this message—accepts all it contains—then man must at last wake out of his milleniary dream and in doing so wake to his total solitude, his fundamental isolation. Now does he at last realize that, like a gypsy he lives on the boundary of an alien world. A world that is deaf to his music, just as indifferent to his hopes as it is to his sufferings or his crimes."[7]

No real past, then; certainly no direction and clearly no purpose. Just chance: pure, blind, free chance. Much of secular science marches to its tune and worships at its altar, reciting litanies very much like those of Monod.

And what of the future? If the past is just a roll of dice, what does the future hold? Entropic doom, perhaps, if we wait long enough. The energy mainsprings of the universe run down inexorably, and everything ought to pass out of existence eventually, vanishing in an ethereal puff of maximized randomness. In a way, I suppose there's a certain justice in it all—from randomness we've come, to randomness we shall go. Or if you don't like the whimper of entropy, try the bang of nuclear holocaust or the agonies

of massive overcrowding, depletion of nonrenewable resources, or global starvation on the spaceship earth.

The scenarios vary, but the theme is always the same. If
ours is a universe in which we are completely alone, the future offers little cause for hope. Ironically, that is the point
Monod seems to make when he concludes *Chance and Necessity* with these words: "Man knows at last that he is alone
in the universe's unfeeling immensity, out of which he
emerged only by chance. His destiny is nowhere spelled
out, nor is his duty. The kingdom above or the darkness
below; it is for him to choose."[8]

But the real irony is, how shall he choose? Or, for that
matter, how is he able even to tell "below" from "above"?
For is it not the case that the values by which we live in the
present rest ultimately on our concepts of the past and the
future? And if it is true that ours is a past without purpose
and a future without hope, how shall we live in the present?
Where are we to get our values and our moral principles?
If there are no absolutes against which we can measure our
actions, how shall we understand what value is? One thing
seems clear: if man sees himself as Monod sees him, values
are up for grabs. Anything can become a value.[9]

Then, of course, it becomes a temptation to define what
ought to be in terms of what already *is.* Monod recognizes
this and is quoted in an interview in the *New York Times*
as saying, "One of the great problems of philosophy is the
relationship between the realm of knowledge and the realm
of values. Knowledge is what *is,* values are what ought to be.
I would say that all traditional philosophies up to and including Marxism have tried to derive the 'ought to' from
the 'is'."[10]

Increasingly, that is what we seem to be doing in our
society as we move further and further from our historic
Judeo-Christian moorings. Thus Kinsey studies human
sexual behavior, and the primary effect of his report is to
suggest that whatever is average behavior is right. The *is*

becomes the *ought to*. The average becomes the norm. So I look up my age on his chart and find that as long as I'm having sexual intercourse 2.4 times per week, I'm right on. He doesn't specify with whom, and I have certain troubles with that 0.4, but at least I know what ought to be! And with modern means of accumulating data, such sociological norms are eminently practicable. That is what Marshall McLuhan is emphasizing when he says that democracy is finished and that we are living in a global village. All we need are enough computers to record what enough people are thinking and doing at any given moment, and that then becomes the value, perhaps even the law of the world.[11]

The only other workable alternative for moral values in such a godless universe would seem to be the development of some sort of decision-making elite. Thus, B. F. Skinner issues an agonized call for a "culture controller."[12] Monod tells us that to achieve a stable-state society will call for "some form of world authority,"[13] and Sir Francis Crick, another Nobel laureate in molecular biology, writes, "Some group of people should decide who should have more children and who should have fewer. You have to decide who is born."[14]

When we hear language like that, bells ought to ring. Here are yet more voices, respected scientific voices, calling for the development of an elite that will set up arbitrary values, arbitrary absolutes to control the world. How many more Thousand-Year Reichs do we need before we recognize such voices for where they ultimately lead?

The problem, of course, is that with man being considered a product of the impersonal plus time plus chance, all values are up for grabs, and we end up with a past with no purpose, a future with no hope, and a present with no real values to live by. And if the picture looks bleak, don't blame me—it's not my picture! It's just the logical, perhaps even inevitable consequence of a world view that recognizes as reality only things that can be observed and measured in a laboratory. A philosophy that places man just a notch above the apes. A naked ape, and nothing more.

Worship at that altar if you must, but know what you're worshiping. Recognize the pit of despair that lies just behind that altar, and listen well to the litany your high priest is chanting: "A world deaf to man's music, indifferent to his hopes. . . . alone in the universe's unfeeling immensity, his destiny nowhere spelled out, nor his duty."

The Alternative

But then know this: *there is an alternative*. You don't have to settle for a world view that begins with nothing but chance and ends with nothing but despair. There *is* an alternative, and it is the Christian Alternative. It says, "Naked ape, yes —but there's more. Man is more than a naked ape, more than a pile of chemicals, more than an information-dense structure. The analytical description may be accurate, but it is not adequate. In the Christian world view, man has a value and a purpose that goes beyond the analytical capacities of science. It is an alternative that begins not with chance but with God. It ends not with despair but with hope. And its litany is the Litany with a Difference! Listen to it, as it flows from the psalmist (8:3-5, 9 NASB):

When I consider Thy heavens, the work of Thy fingers,
The moon and the stars, which Thou hast ordained;
What is man, that Thou dost take thought of him?
And the son of man, that Thou dost care for him?
Yet Thou hast made him a little lower than God,
And dost crown him with glory and majesty! . . .
O LORD, our Lord,
How majestic is Thy name in all the earth!

Quite a difference, isn't there, between the Dirge of Monod and the Hymn of the Psalmist. The difference you hear is the difference of the Christian world view, which I want now to examine.

We begin as we did for the secular world view, by looking

at the presuppositions on which the Christian world view rests. Which means we begin with God, for that is the unique and distinctive feature of the Christian position: it begins with God. If a Christian world view is anything at all, it must begin with the basic idea of a God who exists outside of man, a purposeful, caring God under whom and by whom man and nature were created and apart from whom man can never be fully understood. Notice that this is our axiom. We are not setting out to prove God's existence; we are assuming it. It is our basic presupposition, the basis on which our world view rests.

For many that is the stumbling block. It is apparently easier for many to profess almost unlimited faith in a random collision of atoms than in a caring God. Let me illustrate with an exchange of correspondence from my own file cabinet. A few years ago I was in the midst of correspondence with a publisher who wanted me to write a textbook on cellular biology. Letters had gone back and forth, and we were at the stage where I had received a fairly detailed position paper, laying out their thoughts on the "ideal" cell-biology book as they conceived it. After wading through several pages of detailed descriptions of content and design, I came across this intriguing paragraph under the heading, *Origin of Life:*

Topics to be discussed: cosmology, formation of earth, primeval soup, first cells. This is usually far too briefly discussed, if at all. This text should contain as explicit and detailed an account of the process as the latest findings make possible, including perhaps some frank speculation that would give the student a better handle on the subject, though he should be warned of the uncertainty inherent in studies of life's origins. This discussion could also make clear why God is an unnecessary hypothesis.

I replied with an equally rambling letter, and concluded on page four with the following:

One final point, though: I find myself profoundly disturbed by the comment under item B-4 that "this discussion could also make clear why God is an unnecessary hypothesis." A biology text has a responsibility to present and summarize our current understanding on possible explanations concerning the origin and evolution of life forms, and I would attempt seriously so to do. It has, in my opinion, no right whatever to theological pronouncements which are purported to derive from such a discussion. That a speculative consideration of primeval soup should lead to a summary dismissal of a theistic viewpoint strikes me not only as untenable and irrelevant, but also as sadly absurd. I could in no wise contribute to a textbook which purports to draw theological conclusions from pseudoscientific speculation. You might, by the way, wish to consider the appropriateness of a note of praise that God in His infinite wisdom and patience has not yet seen fit to declare you an unnecessary hypothesis.

The problem, of course, as I indicated, is that the existence of God cannot be deduced from the data—since, in the Christian view, God is the source of the data, and his existence is an essential presupposition. What we *can* do, as with any world view, is to look at the *consequences* of the Christian alternative and see how they compare with what we know or can perceive to be true. To examine some of these consequences, let's look at what the Christian alternative has to say about the past, the future, and the present, in that order.

First, the past. Here we turn not to the chance and necessity of Monod, but to the creative power of a sovereign, caring God. In this, we agree with the writer of Genesis that "in the beginning God created." As Christians, we understand all of the physical universe as the design and creation of God. Thus, when I as a biologist look through the electron microscope into a subcellular world hundreds of thousands of times smaller than I can see with the unaided eye and find myself awed and amazed at the intricacy of design and the marvels of structural integration, I don't have to attribute all that intricacy, all that design and all that order to random events over eons of time. I realize that I am looking directly into the handiwork of an omnipotent God, from whom I have every right to expect intricacy, design, order and purpose.

I am not easily distracted by those who insist that creation and evolution must be viewed as mutually exclusive alternatives. To me, creation by evolution is more helpful than creation versus evolution. To me, the miracle of creation remains a miracle regardless of the time scale by which God worked, especially when I realize that God is timeless, operating outside our dimensions of time and space. For him, the Bible says, a thousand years become as but a day. Whether six days or billions of years, it remains every bit as marvelous. It would, I suppose, be a supreme bit of irony if because of the time span the best of our scientific minds could be fooled into looking at isolated events and claim to see only random chance at work.

Fundamental to the Christian world view, then, is the conviction that all of nature is God's creation. And because God is purposeful and caring, I can search with confidence both to know him as Creator and to discern the purpose and meaning of his creation. In that search, I find myself aided immeasurably by the fact that God has revealed himself not only *in* his creation, but also *to* his creation. Beyond the natural revelation in creation, which I as a scientist count myself privileged to explore, he has revealed himself in human history—first to his chosen people, the people of Israel, and then supremely and personally in the life, death and physical resurrection of Jesus Christ. God continues to reveal himself experientially in the lives of his people, among whom I rejoice to count myself. All of that revelation—natural, historical and experiential—is attested to by biblical documents whose authenticity and reliability are beyond serious challenge (Prof. Schoville will discuss that elsewhere in this book).

If anything whatsoever is clear in all of God's revelation, it is this: man occupies a distinctive position in creation. Man is not merely a part of nature, not merely a naked ape. He is that, to be sure, but he is more. When you are all done describing man as an animal, you are not yet finished—in the Christian view. There is something further, something more. The ultimate meaning of man lies outside himself. It is to be found in his relationship to the God who has created him and who calls him into fellowship.

Man exists as a distinctive object of God's creation, and can be adequately understood only in that context. The Bible's way of putting it is that man is "created in the image of God." Prof. Wilkes has already paraphrased that for us by saying that man is capable of receiving communication from God and exchanging communication with God, and that is a phenomenon you cannot measure in the scientific laboratory. Man is only one end of a conversation, and you will never fully understand the conversation by analyzing only one end of it.

So far, then, we have two unique and tremendously significant features of the Christian alternative: a *past* characterized not by random chance and blind accident but by the direction and purpose to be expected of a creative God, and a *view of man* that moves beyond being a naked ape to being made in the image of God.

And if that is the past, what can we say of the future? Simply this. It is a future with a hope. If the universe has been called into being by a purposeful God, and if we are created in his image to share in his nature, then surely all of this is going somewhere. That, too, is part of God's revelation. Indeed, it is the most glorious part of that revelation. We are given to understand that, however dimly we may at times perceive it, all of history is moving not toward entropic doom or global catastrophe, but toward a future that culminates in the reign of Jesus Christ as King of kings and Lord of lords. It is a reign in which all of his people will share.

Now don't misunderstand that hope as some kind of airy-fairy, pie-in-the-sky dream. The Christian is painfully aware of the multitude of problems threatening the quality and even the existence of life here on earth. Indeed, the Christian ought if anything to be more concerned than most people about the bettering of human society. Such Christian concern has been borne out again and again in history, including the history of higher education. But the real hope of the Christian alternative lies not in any sort of utopian human society, but in the firm conviction that, ultimately, our citizenship is not of this world. Ours is a future with the stamp of eternity on it, sealed by the historical fact of the resurrection of Jesus Christ and by the promise that because he lives, we too shall live.

The Choice

The Christian alternative, then, offers a past with a purpose that is rooted in God and a future with a hope that is grounded in eternity. That past and that future in turn have real bearing on the present. We have a present with both a sense of direction to move in and a set of values to move by. We have direction because we know where we've come from and where we're going. We see God's purpose at work in the past. We know something of his ultimate plan for the future. We sense his guidance in the present. We have values to live by because he has, in his revelations to his people, shown us the moral principles by which we are to be guided. As Christians we ought not (indeed we dare not) grope about for societal norms, hoping to find what ought to be in what is. Nor need we join in agonized calls for cultural controllers or elitist authority. By the Christian perspective we are created in God's image to live by his precepts, and we are enabled to do so by the power of his indwelling Spirit.

This, then, is the Christian alternative to the secular view that looks on man as little more than naked ape. Instead of blind chance and random change, we see the purposeful, creative hand of God. Instead of seeing doom and catastrophe ahead, we look to a future that culminates in the reign of Jesus Christ. Instead of groping for values among arid human philosophies, we find them in the revealed will of God. Instead of despairing of a world that is, in Monod's words, "deaf to our music and as indifferent to our hopes as it is to our sufferings," we rejoice in a God who listens for our music, who cares about our hopes and who shares in our sufferings so intimately that he came among us in the person of Jesus Christ to make our sufferings his own.

In the light of all this, the Christian alternative sees man as he was really intended to be: not just a naked ape to be studied and described, not just a collection of chemicals to be analyzed and priced, not just an accident whose number came up, but the object of God's creative power. To live in everlasting fellowship with our Creator, we must realize that what some dismiss as an "unnecessary hypothesis" is in reality the only presupposition worth staking our life on.

So the two altars stand today, as in Old Testament times they did on Mt. Carmel. The voice of the prophet still echoes over them, "How long will you hesitate between two opinions?"

The altar on the left is labeled "secular world view." The one on the right is labeled "Christian alternative." The former recognizes as reality only things that can be observed and measured in the laboratory. The latter recognizes value and purpose that lie beyond. The former sees man as a naked ape; the latter, as the image of God. The former calls us to believe that beyond the physical universe and the natural world lies nothing. The latter summons us to confess that beyond the physical universe and the natural world God *is*. Make no mistake about it. Both require acts of faith.

Listen once again to the litanies, and then choose your altar carefully—because much of what you are, or ever will become, depends on the altar at which you worship.

First, from the altar on the left, the words of Jacques Monod:

Chance alone is at the source of every innovation, of all creation in the biosphere. Pure chance, absolutely free, but blind. . . . Man knows at last that he is alone in the universe's unfeeling immensity. His destiny is nowhere spelled out, nor is his duty.[15]

And from the altar on the right, these words from the prophet Isaiah: (42:5-6 NASB)

Thus says God the LORD,

Who created the heavens and stretched them out,

Who spread out the earth and its offspring,

Who gives breath to the people on it,

And spirit to those who walk in it,

"I am the Lord, I have called you in righteousness,

I will also hold you by the hand and watch over you."

Those are the litanies, those the altars. The choice before you is clear.

Notes
[1]D. Morris, *The Naked Ape* (New York: Dell, 1967).
[2]Ibid., p. 9.
[3]H. J. Morowitz, "The High Cost of Being Human," *New York Times,* 11 Feb. 1979, p. 41.
[4]J. Monod, *Chance and Necessity* (New York: A. A. Knopf, 1971).
[5]Ibid., pp. 112-13.
[6]F. Schaeffer, *Back to Freedom and Dignity* (Downers Grove: InterVarsity Press, 1972).
[7]Monod, pp. 172-73.
[8]Ibid., p. 180.
[9]Schaeffer, p. 14.
[10]J. Monod, quoted by J. C. Hess, *New York Times,* 15 Mar. 1971, p. 6.
[11]Schaeffer, p. 15.
[12]B. F. Skinner, *Beyond Freedom and Dignity* (New York: A. A. Knopf, 1971).
[13]Monod, quoted by Hess, p. 6.
[14]F. Crick, "Why I Study Biology," a lecture delivered in St. Louis (March 1971) and quoted by Schaeffer, pp. 16-22.
[15]Monod, *Chance and Necessity,* pp. 112, 180.

Recommended Reading
Monod, J. *Chance and Necessity.* New York: A. A. Knopf, 1971.
Morris, D. *The Naked Ape.* New York: Dell, 1967.
Schaeffer, F. A. *Back to Freedom and Dignity.* Downers Grove: Inter-Varsity Press, 1972.
————————————————. *Genesis in Space and Time.* Downers Grove: InterVarsity Press, 1972.
Skinner, B. F. *Beyond Freedom and Dignity.* New York: A. A. Knopf, 1971.

Chapter 4
Christian Doubts about Economic Dogmas

J. David Richardson

W hat is meant by "The Christian Alternative to Secular Dogma" in the sphere of economics? What does economics believe which could in any way be construed as an alternative to Christian belief? My answer is threefold and will serve to outline my talk.[1]

First, economics has views on the nature of man that are shared in common by most economists worldwide but differ from Christian views.

Second, economics has views on the desirability of certain "economic systems" (a term I will define later) which can be classified broadly along a continuum from individualist to collectivist systems. In Christian belief, however, far more important than the systems themselves are economic relationships among individuals and groups *within* an economic system.

Third, some economic historians, commentators and a

group of people we might call economic humanists have charged that the Christian faith (especially in the West) has been used to justify attitudes toward work, property and the environment which have caused significant injury and suffering. To that indictment the Christian must respond that the Christian faith has not been *used* to justify those attitudes, but *ab*used.

Economic Man
What is the economist's view of the nature of man? It is this: A person's economic well-being depends on the amount of goods and services at his or her personal command; each person's goal is to achieve maximal personal economic well-being. Thus the creature whom we call "economic man" is materialistic, egocentric and immoderate (or you might say just plain greedy).

Now believe it or not, Christians *can* accept that as a useful characterization of human beings in their actions before they have encountered and surrendered to the living, loving God. But Christians reject it as a *complete* characterization of humanity. Even unredeemed persons are not *just* materialistic, egocentric, immoderate and nothing more. As Jesus himself said, quoting the Old Testament, "Man cannot live on bread alone" (Mt. 4:4; Deut. 8:3—both TEV). Of course careful economists also reject "economic man" as a complete characterization of the nature of man— because careful economists recognize the inability of the logic called economics to explain *all* human behavior. Even so, we have had a spate of articles lately on the economics of crime, cheating and lying, child production, extramarital affairs and even, in a recent textbook, a chapter called "Dying: The Most Economical Way to Go."

Christians go even further than careful economists in rejecting "economic man" as an adequate characterization of human nature. Christians believe that even if you could devise an economic system that would finally make all individuals materially prosperous by their own definitions—including among material things child production, extramarital affairs, method of dying and so on—you would not thereby have made them happy. Nor would you necessarily have made them happier than they were before they became prosperous. Christians believe that the only lasting happiness comes from drawing close to the living, loving God through Jesus Christ, whom Scripture calls "the exact likeness of God's own being" (Heb. 1:3 TEV). And when men and women draw close to God through Jesus Christ, he inhabits them in such a way that the most important things to them in life are *not* material anymore. They are able to look *beyond themselves* to other men and women around them, see them through God's eyes and love them in imitation of his love ("as they love their own selves," the Bible says). For a Christian, the whole materialistic, egocentric, immoderate nature of man is replaced by a *new nature.*

Economic Systems

A second area in which Christians may disagree with economics has to do with "economic systems," by which I mean institutional structures within which economic men and women conduct their business. In fact, economists disagree among themselves on the desirability of alternative economic systems. Even economists will admit that *this* aspect of the field cannot be value free.

On the far right within economics are the defenders of "economic individualism." That system, in which every man and woman is free to compete in a marketplace, features voluntary action. Prices, and not the policy decisions of any government or bureaucracy, determine the allocation of privately owned resources to various economic activities. Prices determine the amount of production and the distribution of that production to members of the society, who then own it privately as individuals. Defenders of economic individualism are able to show that under certain conditions, an economic system based on private property, markets and voluntary transactions maximizes the material goods available to the system as a whole.

Defenders of "economic collectivism," the opposing perspective within economics, doubt the realism of those conditions.

What *really* happens, say the defenders of collectivism, is that systems based on markets, private property and competition invariably produce a large set of "losers"—people who are forced into *in*voluntary action by the individualism of others. Losers don't have the strength, wealth, position, intelligence or aggressiveness that "winners" have. The result for the losers is a cycle of indignity, weakness, dependence, poverty and exploitation that leads to alienation from the winners, and to bitterness, sullenness and lack of self-respect. That vicious circle is perpetuated from generation to generation.

That circle, in the eyes of collectivists, can be immoral. The losers are in a sense disenfranchised by the individualistic market system. The so-called freedom inherent in an extreme individualistic market system could equally well be described as "license," or as "freedom to exploit."

In a collectivist economic system, the vicious circle is broken in principle by having a representative government to overrule, and maybe even replace markets, in order to assure a "fair" distribution of wealth, consumption, position and education.

We can immediately see the awkward problem in collectivism of deciding what is *fair*. This is a moral problem which Christians do not believe that people on their own have the right to solve. But we see just as clearly the equally awkward identification in economic individualism of *fairness* with what the system actually produces—that is, the identification of what *should be* with what *is,* which Christians reject, as Prof. Becker made clear in the preceding lecture.

So what *do* Christians believe about economic systems? It seems at first blush to depend on where in the world those Christians live. Many Christians in the U.S. and Canada feel strongly that Christianity and systems of economic individualism go together hand in hand. Radical Christians, a minority worldwide, feel strongly that Christianity and systems of economic collectivism go together hand in hand. Both groups of Christians support their views adamantly and stridently and cite appropriate biblical passages to buttress them.

But I am afraid that both have "added to the Christian faith" what does not belong—in a way that Scripture explicitly prohibits. The Bible itself holds out with approval primitive models of *both* economic individualism *and* economic collectivism. With reference to individualism, much of Jewish law, beginning with "thou shalt not steal," revolves around private rights and conduct in the marketplace for private employers of labor, private lenders of financial capital, individual farmers and individual merchants. With reference to collectivism, Scripture records how Joseph nationalized production and property during the great Egyptian famine (Gen. 47:13-26). It records that the early Christian church in Jerusalem held all property and goods collectively, distributing it among themselves under the direction of governing apostles and deacons "as any had need" (Acts 2:43-47; 4:32-35; 6:1-7). That scriptural phrase, incidentally, reappears in the writings of Karl Marx.

The Bible, which Christians believe to be God's own word, is also evenhanded in its disapproval of certain aspects of economic systems. It indicts economic exploitation of the weak by the strong under economic individualism as well as exploitation of the governed by the economic governors under economic collectivism (Eccles. 5:8; Ezek. 22:25, 27; 34:1-10). This discussion reveals that the most important economic imperatives in the Christian faith relate to the ways that individuals treat individuals and the

ways that groups treat groups under *any* economic system
—wherever it lies along the continuum between individualism and collectivism.

For example, the economically strong and rich are specifically enjoined again and again through Scripture to provide for the economically weak and poor. Creditors are specifically forbidden to deprive debtors of clothing or the
means of livelihood as collateral for loans; they are instructed to cancel all debts every seven years. Employers are
specifically enjoined from depriving employees of just
wages. Slaves are instructed to "work heartily" for their
masters (Col. 3:23), as if their master were God himself.
Slave owners are reminded that they themselves are like
slaves to the Master/Creator (Col. 4:1) and must treat their
slaves with the same love and provision that God has shown
to them.

A Christian hopes and prays that such biblical economic
imperatives for *relationships* will be observed in every
economic *system.* Simultaneously, a Christian doubts that
the economic morality which God ordains will be brought
about more or less predictably by *any* particular economic
system or any economic set of institutions.

The Work Ethic
That brings us to the third area in which Christians and
some secular economists disagree. The Christian faith is
sometimes castigated by secular commentators for creating
and defending a "work ethic" in which material wealth and
prosperity are the direct rewards for economic ambition
and diligence. Even if that work ethic sounds okay, the
other side of the coin is that material poverty and destitution are then the direct result of indolence and sloth. The
sinister implications of the so-called Christian work ethic
(say the commentators) are undeniable. First, property becomes the *right* of the propertied classes, no matter how
attained; "he who violates my property violates my rights."

Second, poverty becomes the "just deserts" of the impoverished; "if only they were more ambitious and more diligent they would rise from poverty." A third sinister implication, say these commentators, is that nature itself is seen as private property, to be polluted, defoliated and made extinct as the propertied classes see fit.

Too all those accusations a Christian responds a resounding "not guilty." If we are sensitive Christians, we do so repentantly, however, recognizing that we are partially responsible if we ever allow *abusers* of the Christian faith to claim its sanction and power without our strong challenge. It is really abuse of the faith on which the secular view is focused.

In the matter of indolence and the work ethic, the Christian faith is not what the secular view thinks. Admittedly, Scripture is clear on the inevitable consequences of laziness. But Scripture is equally clear (a) that there is *no* salvation through hard work or effort; (b) that material wealth and prosperity are often *not* the direct results of diligence or ambition, but rather a freely given gift of God to those whom he chooses to bless with them; and (c) that people are often *not* responsible for their own poverty and destitution. Often they have inherited it from earlier generations or have been victimized by the economic manipulation and aggression of the rich and strong.

The writer of Proverbs said: "Be wise enough not to wear yourself out trying to get rich. Your money can be gone in a flash, as if it had grown wings and flown away like an eagle" (23:4 TEV). The writer of Ecclesiastes said: "I have . . . learned why people work so hard to succeed: it is because they envy the things their neighbors have. But it is useless. It is like chasing the wind . . . it is better to have only a little, with peace of mind, than be busy all the time with both hands, trying to catch the wind" (4:4-6 TEV). The writer of the Epistle to the Hebrews said: "Keep your lives free from the love of money, and be satisfied with what you have. For God has said, 'I will never leave you; I will never abandon you' " (13:5 TEV). And Jesus Christ said, "Watch out and guard yourself from every kind of greed; because a person's life is not made up of the things he owns, no matter how rich he may be" (Lk. 12:15 TEV).

What is the Christian response to the secular accusation that Christians feel that all their property is theirs by right? The Christian answer is that all property is the Lord's. We are at best only temporary stewards of it under his watchful eyes and under his ultimate judgment. The psalmist said, "The earth is the Lord's, and everything in it, the world, and all who live in it" (24:1 NIV). The apostle Paul made personal application of that divine-ownership claim even more graphic in his first letter to the Corinthians (6:19-20 TEV): even one's own body is not one's property, he said. "You do not belong to yourselves but to God; he bought you for a price." And Moses predated both by declaring, "To the LORD belong even the highest heavens; the earth is his also, and everything on it" (Deut. 10:14 TEV).

C. S. Lewis, the late British medievalist and Christian apologist, expanded on these biblical themes in an engaging way in the *Screwtape Letters,* which might be regarded as a set of professorial lecture notes for distribution to all students—only the professor is a satanic scholar and the student is a junior devil.

Here is what the satanic scholar says to his young advisee:

> The sense of ownership in general is always to be encouraged. The humans are always putting up claims to ownership which sound equally funny in Heaven and in Hell, and we must keep them doing so. Much of the modern resistance to chastity comes from men's belief that they "own" their bodies. . . . It is as if a royal child whom his father has placed, for love's sake, in titular command of some great province, under the real rule of wise counsellors, should come to fancy he really owns the

cities, the forests, and the corn, in the same way as he owns the bricks on the nursery floor. . . .

And all the time the joke is that the word "mine" in its fully possessive sense cannot be uttered by a human about anything. In the long run either Our Father [Satan] or the Enemy [God] will say "mine" of each thing that exists, and specially of each man. They will find out in the end, never fear, to whom their time, their souls, and their bodies really belong—certainly not to *them,* whatever happens. At present the Enemy [God] says "mine" of everything on the pedantic, legalistic ground that He made it. Our Father [Satan] hopes in the end to say "mine" of all things on the more realistic and dynamic ground of conquest.[2]

Some Christians may mistakenly think that the Lord's injunction to "subdue the earth" (Gen. 1:28) provides some justification for despoiling and destroying the environment, or may mistakenly think that the animal kingdom is to be exploited and disposed of at human whim. They should be reminded of the words spoken by the psalmist about God himself: "You show your care for the land by sending rain"; "Men and animals are in your care" (65:9; 36:6 TEV). It is sobering to remember that God found his created universe *good* and it is not our place to destroy it, but God's.

I have been speaking extensively of the *biblical* imperatives for economic behavior and economic relationships because a Christian goes to the Bible as the primary source of God's revealed will for humankind. In the next lecture Prof. Keith Schoville from the university's department of Hebrew and Semitic studies will discuss the desirability of using the Bible that way, and why it can be trusted.

A Christian Alternative
So far I've made Christian economic imperatives an alternative to secular economic imperatives, but not necessarily

a *compelling* alternative.

As Prof. Becker stated, however, we are taking part in this lecture series because we find Christianity compelling as an alternative to secular dogma. The most important reason we find it compelling is that a Christian *can* answer the question, "Why *this* system of economic values and not some other?" The answer is, because the Christian set of economic values is based through and through on the principle, "Love your neighbor as you love yourself." Of course so are some other systems of values. But they, unlike Christianity, rarely have an answer to the awkward further question, "Why *should* I love my neighbor as I love myself?" The Christian answer to that question is this: because God loves your neighbor and insists that we as Christians see as much in our neighbor as he himself does.

The Bible teaches that God is *every* man's and *every* woman's suitor. His love is not always returned, but when it is, and an "engagement" takes place, there is rejoicing in heaven and on earth. The implication of God's "courtship" of human beings for Christian economic morality (and for any other social morality) is that God will be as enraged as any suitor or fiancé when we mistreat the ones he loves. His love is essentially the same for the nonbelievers he courts as for the believers he plans to "wed." Hence our Christian economic conduct should be essentially the same toward non-Christians as it is toward Christians.

Further, God's potential anger if we disobey is only one factor that motivates Christian social and economic morality. The other is his plan that his love should *inhabit us,* that we should be transformed by his indwelling presence to become suitors and fiancés ourselves of all other men and women—because we want to, not because we have to.

What do Christians mean when they say "God *loves* all men and women?" The Bible answers that in the book of Colossians in beautiful *economic* terminology: "You were at one time spiritually dead because of your sins. . . . But God has now brought you to life with Christ. God forgave us all our sins; he canceled the unfavorable record of our debts . . . and did away with it completely by nailing it to the cross" (2:13-14 TEV).

My wish for each of you is that you have seen or will see the heavy ledger of your debts to God nailed to the cross of Jesus, so that he bears the weight of that ledger, canceling your debt. That is why he came—in love.

Notes

[1] I would like to express thanks to John Dodge, one of our graduate students, for his critical input into this discussion, and for a very useful set of bibliographical references.

[2] C. S. Lewis, *Screwtape Letters* (New York: Macmillan, 1961), pp. 97-99.

Recommended Reading

Catherwood, H. F. R. *The Christian in Industrial Society.* Rev. ed. Leicester: Inter-Varsity Press, 1980.

Harrower, John D. *Economics–A Christian Perspective,* No. 4 in Zadok Centre Series No. 1, monograph, March 1978 (Address: 4 Ryrie Street, Campbell ACT 2601, Australia).

Munby, D. L. *Christianity and Economic Problems.* London: Macmillan, 1956.

Vickers, Douglas. *Economics and Man.* Nutley, N.J.: Craig Press, 1976.

Chapter 5
The Reliability
of the
Scriptural Documents

Keith Schoville

I am part of the faculty of the humanities division of the College of Letters and Science. The humanities are concerned with art, architecture, history, philosophy and literature, among other things. Since literature is one of the humanistic concerns, and since I work with literature, it seems appropriate that I should speak about the Bible, the fundamental literature—in terms of pervasive influence— of western civilization.

More specifically, I want to discuss the historical reliability of the scriptural documents because in our contemporary society there is a widely held viewpoint, a dogma if you will, that the Bible is irrelevant to the needs of humanity.

Secular Dogma
Today's secular dogma about the unreliability of the Bible appears in three basic forms: in modern critical scholarship, in atheistic humanism and among indifferent individuals.

Modern critical biblical scholarship. The late eighteenth and the nineteenth centuries saw the rise of a modern critical study of the Bible. At the heart of such scholarship is the idea that the Bible can be approached as an essentially human document from the ancient past and can be treated to the same critical methods of study as those used on the ancient classics of Greece and Rome. That means that literary scholars would attempt to apply the methodology of science to the biblical documents. We do not have the time nor is it our purpose here to review the history of modern critical biblical scholarship. What I want to note is that the scholar who uses this approach treats the Bible as an ancient artifact to be studied and analyzed as an academic exercise. Supposedly, the Bible is to be studied in a detached, objective manner. It is seen as an interesting but ancient religious document with little or no contemporary relevance.

The Bible, in that view, is regarded as the word of human writers but not as the Word of God—for everyone knows that there is no place for God in our wonderful, modern world, where the happiness and fulfillment of every individual is assured because of the inherent benevolence of human nature!

Atheistic humanism. Another manifestation of the secular dogma sees the Bible as a dangerous document, because it is in opposition to what certain individuals believe is best for human beings. Perhaps the outstanding representative of that "humanist" viewpoint is Madalyn Murray O'Hair. As an atheist, O'Hair does not believe in the existence of God. In her 1972 book, *The Atheist Viewpoint,* she states her belief that "Jesus Christ was either a man or a myth." She goes on to affirm that "As history and science both deny that the stories told of him can be true, we stand on firm ground in asserting the myth theory."[1]

O'Hair quotes with enthusiasm the words of another atheist, Patrick Campbell. He states that "There is not a tittle [a biblical allusion] of evidence that such a man as

Moses ever lived, yet these historically worthless books are actually the literary foundation of Christianity. The critical study of the Bible has hopelessly shattered the authority for the study of Jesus Christ no less than for the account of Moses. The Higher Criticism has demonstrated that the Gospels were written long after the supposed time of Christ. These conflicting and false Gospel stories, concerning which nobody knows who wrote a single line, or how often they were subsequently rewritten, tell the all-too-recognizable pagan fable of a man or a God whose father was a Holy Ghost and whose mother was a Virgin, a man who performed miracles, cast devils out of fellow beings, and even raised the dead."[2]

Campbell goes on to deride the miracles of healing recorded in the Gospels and closes by stating, "Be that all as it may, the story of the crucifixion in itself is sufficient to deny the miracles Jesus is said to have performed and to deny that he was God."[3]

O'Hair concludes her questioning of the proofs of the historicity of Jesus with the statement that "Jesus, like all gods of old, is gone, and there is no evidence or reason for supposing that he was ever any more of a reality than his countless predecessors."[4]

Of a similar stuff are the words of a certain Robert F. Bartley, who published a book in 1979 entitled *The Star-studded Hoax of Christianity with its Allied Gods.* He maintains that Jesus Christ is a myth who never existed because he was never born. Therefore, the Lord Jesus Christ is one of the greatest hoaxes ever foisted upon civilization. "The solution of the supposed birth of Jesus Christ begins with Paul, because history never heard the name of Jesus Christ until Paul came along to write about it. Paul was the inventor of Jesus Christ and Christianity."[5]

In another section of his book Bartley states that Moses could have written only in cuneiform, since, he says, the alphabet "as we know it was invented by the Phoenicians about B.C. 1000, or approximately 500 years after the death of Moses."[6]

What these statements point out, apart from the ignorance of the individuals who made them concerning historical facts, is that the secular world view has eliminated God and the Bible as a myth.

Indifferent individuals. The third manifestation of the secular dogma is probably the most insidious. It is the millions of people, many of them professing to be religious, both Christians and Jews, who ignore the Bible. We meet them, some of them among faculty, students and administrators here on the campus everyday.

As pertains to the Bible, then, the secular world has eliminated God so that the Bible is viewed as an antiquated curio or collection of dangerous myths—or is simply not noticed at all. The Christian alternative to those secular dogmas is that *the biblical documents are reliable.* We can take the Bible seriously.

Why Respect the Bible?
The Bible is worthy of serious and respectful attention because of its antiquity, remarkable survival, historicity and contemporaneity.

The special nature of the Bible's antiquity: its homogeneity. Of all of the literatures that have come down to us from the past, the Bible represents the oldest homogeneous collection. There are older literatures; for example, we have extant materials from the ancient Sumerians, the earliest of civilizations. Sumerian literary materials date to approximately 2500 B.C., a millennium after that civilization began to develop. We also have literary materials from the ancient Egyptians, Babylonians, Assyrians, Hittites and Canaanites. These are all older literatures than what we have in the Bible, but we have them only piecemeal. They are not homogeneous.

It is true that in the Bible we have a diversity of literary materials. Yet it is also true that the Bible from beginning to end is permeated by a basic unity about the nature of God and the nature of man. The Bible possesses remarkable homogeneity.

And we should recall there that the Bible is the literature of a people who were never great and powerful. The great empires have come and gone, and their literatures have come down to us by happenstance, while the spiritual heirs of ancient Israel have survived the ebb and flow of history, as has the literature which we have in the Bible.

I believe that the unity of the Bible is due to the world view of the writers, a world view that was unique in its time, an extraordinary break with past religious traditions. The mindset of the various hands that participated in the writing of the biblical literature focused on the realities of human existence in a believable, rational way. Further, that focus lasted not just for a single generation but continued across at least a millennium of time. Thus, despite the diversity of authorship, the varied backgrounds of the writers, the variety of purposes which they pursued in their writing and the different periods in which each of them worked, the Bible exhibits a unique homogeneity in comparison to the other literatures of the ancient world.

The Bible's remarkable survival. We ought to treat the Bible with more than average respect also because it is the oldest continuously surviving body of ancient literature.

On the shelves of my library, and available to you on the shelves of the libraries of this university, are collections and translations of the other ancient literatures I have mentioned. They can be read in English translation. They have survived in part by chance. They have been recovered to a large degree by accident; they did not survive purposefully. The Bible, on the other hand, has been preserved continuously, not by accident, but purposefully.

Could we use here a modern, scientific explanation for that phenomenon? Could it not be an example of "the survival of the fittest"?

On the other hand, no other collection of ancient literature has suffered such intense efforts to stamp it out. Over 2,200 years ago a Syrian king determined to eliminate Judaism from his realm, which included the area of ancient Palestine. A contemporary account of the effort is recorded in 1 Maccabees. The writer reports that "All scrolls of the law which were found were torn up and burnt. Anyone discovered in possession of a Book of the Covenant, or conforming to the law, was put to death by the king's sentence" (1:56-57).

In another instance, during the reign of the emperor Diocletian (A.D. 303-305), Christians were forbidden to gather together, and an imperial edict was published everywhere ordering that "churches be razed to the ground, that Scriptures be destroyed by fire." No wonder devout Christians and Jews have earned the title, "the People of the Book."

The Bible has survived its attackers. In our own time the regimes of communist states by and large view the Bible as a threat to their countries' stability. They hamper the widespread dissemination of the Bible among their citizens. I have on my desk a note that the Russians arrested Joseph Bondarenko on May 9, 1978. He had been an active preacher and Christian leader. Before his arrest he called attention to the tremendous need for Bibles in Russia. Fifty million people in Russia would like to have a Bible, but no bookstores will stock it. It is still revolutionary literature because it provides a radical alternative to communist orthodoxy. It is one of the most difficult books to acquire in communist countries, which are known for their use of the printing press for propagandistic publications.

The Bible's remarkable historicity. We ought to take the Bible seriously because its essential historicity has been established.

The framework of ancient history, in fact, is based on the

biblical evidence, modified and embellished by other non-biblical evidence that continues to be recovered in archaeological excavations in the lands of the Bible.

With the development of modern archaeological research, some extraordinary discoveries have been made that indicate the historical authenticity of the Bible. In giving the following examples that support the essential historicity of particular items in the Bible, I am primarily concerned with the Hebrew Bible, the Old Testament. I have chosen to do that not because the historicity of the New Testament documents is questionable; on the contrary, they are more firmly established as authentically historical than any other ancient documents from the classical world. For a clear presentation of the information supporting the historicity of the New Testament texts, consult F. F. Bruce's *The New Testament Documents: Are They Reliable?* First published in 1943, when Bruce was just beginning his distinguished career, the fifth edition, thoroughly revised, was published in January 1960. Now recently retired from his post as Rylands professor of biblical criticism and exegesis at the University of Manchester in England, he has published an essay in a recent issue of *Christianity Today* entitled "Are the New Testament Documents Still Reliable?"[7] The answer is yes.

Professor Bruce notes that archaeological research continues to provide pieces of evidence bearing on the New Testament record. An example is the 1961 discovery at Caesarea Maritin of a stone bearing the name of Pontius Pilate. This is the only extant inscriptional reference to Pilate.

Also at Caesarea in 1962 a fragmentary Hebrew inscription was discovered. It is engraved on a marble tablet, and lists the twenty-four priestly courses (compare 1 Chron. 24:3-19), with a note of the places in Galilee where the members of each course lived after the destruction of the temple in Jerusalem by the Romans in A.D. 70.

The eighteenth course, Happizzez (1 Chron. 24:15), is

assigned to Nazareth. Although the place-name Nazareth occurs in Greek in the Gospels and in subsequent Christian literature, this inscription is the earliest-known occurrence in Hebrew. Before the 1962 find, the earliest was a reference in a *piyyut,* a liturgical poem, of the eleventh century A.D.

F. F. Bruce provides much more information in his book and in his recent article. For those who are interested, I recommend that you read them in detail.

But what about the authenticity of the Hebrew Bible, the Old Testament, in light of the statements above made by the atheists Campbell, Bartley and O'Hair? Since the development of modern archaeological research in the past century or so, discovery after discovery has been made that supports the authenticity of the history in the Bible.

As long ago as 1868, a German missionary by the name of Klein came across an engraved stone in Transjordan, in the region once inhabited by the ancient Moabites. Now known as the Meshe Stele or the Moabite Stone, it contains an account of the exploits of Mesha, king of Moab, and dates to approximately 830 B.C. Mesha is mentioned in 2 Kings 3:5. "When Ahab died, the king of Moab rebelled against the king of Israel." The Moabite Stone contains an extrabiblical account of that conflict.

From the ruins of cities in ancient Mesopotamia a host of documents has been recovered that bear on the historicity of the Bible and authenticate it. 2 Kings 18:17 reports that "In the fourteenth year of the reign of Hezekiah [this was in the days of the prophet Isaiah, about 702 B.C.], Sennacherib, king of Assyria, attacked and took all the fortified cities of Judah. Hezekiah, king of Judah, sent a message to the king of Assyria at Lachish: 'I have done wrong; withdraw from my land, and I will pay any penalty you may impose upon me.' " Sennacherib's annals have been recovered from the ruins of his palace at Nineveh. They do not mention his capture of the city of Lachish, but a bas-relief adorning the entrance to his throne room depicted the Assyrian king sitting on the throne in his camp outside the conquered city of Lachish, surrounded by his officers. Representatives of the stricken town pay homage to him, and captives, including women and children, are led past him.

Sennacherib then went on to lay siege to Jerusalem itself. At that time Hezekiah prepared for the siege by building a secret tunnel under a hill in Jerusalem to carry water from the spring Gihon to the pool of Siloam, hidden within his city walls. The siege began but was never completed. The biblical writers attribute the lifting of the siege to God's activity; the Assyrian records do not record a reason, but the city is not listed as captured. Yet the Assyrian record established the essential validity of the biblical account in these words:

> But as for Hezekiah, the Jew, who did not bow in submission to my yoke, forty-six of his strong walled towns and innumerable smaller villages in their neighborhood I besieged and conquered by stamping down earth-ramps and then bringing up battering rams, by the assault of foot-soldiers, by breaches, tunnelling and sapper operations. I made to come out from them 200,150 people, young and old, male and female, innumerable horses, mules, donkeys, camels, large and small cattle, and counted them as the spoils of war. He himself I shut up like a caged bird within Jerusalem, his royal city.[8]

On March 15 and 16, 597 B.C., Nebuchadnezzar, king of Babylon, captured the city of Jerusalem. That capture is recorded in a tablet now resting in the British Museum. The tablet substantiates the prophecy of Jeremiah and his account of the fall of Jerusalem (Jer. 38—39). A decade later the Babylonians returned to destroy the rebellious city.

From the same Babylonian Chronicle we have a secular account of the fall of Babylon to the Medes and the Persians (mentioned in Dan. 5:30-31).

Some of the discoveries I have mentioned have been

known for a considerable period of time, but more recent discoveries have further authenticated the historical memory of the Bible. Consider the recent discoveries at Tell Mardikh in Syria. That site contains the ruins of an ancient city called Ebla. Since 1973 Italian archaeologists have been recovering cuneiform texts that go back to the Sargonic period or earlier, about 2400-2250 B.C. Over 20,000 tablets have been found thus far. About 20 per cent of the tablets are in a language which has been called paleo-Canaanite, with strong affinities to later Hebrew and Phoenician. Among those tablets are economic texts that include the names of places within Syria/Palestine, with which the Eblaites carried on trade. Those tablets antedate the Old Testament patriarch Abraham by at least 500 years.

In Genesis 14 we have an account of a group of cities that were located in the region of the Dead Sea. Five cities are mentioned: Sodom, Gomorrah, Admah, Zeboiim and Zoar. Because of certain peculiarities in the fourteenth chapter of Genesis, many scholars have considered the existence of these cities as mythical. Early indications are that the towns are not only mentioned in the texts from Ebla, but are listed in the exact order of the Bible. If that reading of the texts is verified, it would again point to the amazing historical accuracy of the Bible—since the traditions about Abraham were not written down for centuries after his existence, yet the names of these cities would be proven to be authentic on the basis of extrabiblical evidence.

In Numbers 22—24, Balaam, a non-Israelite prophet, was ordered by the king of Moab in Transjordan to curse the invading Israelites. Instead, through God's intervention, Balaam blessed them. In 1967, at Tell Deir-'Alla in Jordan, curses of Balaam from other situations were found inscribed on a stele which the archaeologists date to the sixth century B.C.

Recent discoveries also confirm the conservation and conservatism with which the texts were transmitted. The

Dead Sea scrolls from Qumran indicate that the process of transmission was much more complicated than was previously supposed; we find at least three somewhat variant text types in those manuscripts. But at the same time we have a complete copy of the book of Isaiah which is a thousand years older than the previously known oldest copy, and the two are practically identical.

In the middle of the nineteenth century, Count Constantine Tischendorf discovered in St. Catherine's monastery at the foot of Mount Sinai an ancient biblical manuscript, now called Codex Sinaiticus. It was written in the fourth century of this era and stands second only to Codex Vaticanus in age and importance. Those two codices are the chief sources for the New Testament text today, although there are thousands of fragments of other manuscripts for use in comparative studies. According to a 1977 report in the *Biblical Archaeologist,* additional pages of what appear to be missing pages from Codex Sinaiticus have been found at St. Catherine.[9] Other early manuscripts are included in the discovery, although it will be some time before we can know the exact nature of that find.

I do not want to give the false impression that no problems exist in the correlation of data derived from archaeological research with data in the Bible. Yet such problems lie more in the area of the inexactness of archaeology and in the area of interpretation than in the material provided by the biblical documents. One of the great archaeologists and biblical scholars of our time has emphasized the essential historicity of the biblical documents. W. F. Albright was a professor at Johns Hopkins University until his retirement. He died early in the last decade. In his work *History, Archaeology and Christian Humanism* he states:

> We have already seen that archaeological evidence throws its weight squarely against the aberrations of evolutionary historicism as found in most modern literary and historical criticism of the Old and New Testaments.

Yet such critical analyses and even critical excesses have been useful in drawing attention to historical details or phases of development which might otherwise have remained undetected. After the criticism of the last century we can no longer treat Biblical history as naively as was once possible, though we now recognize the substantial historicity of the entire Scriptural tradition from the Patriarchs to the end of the New Testament period.[10]

Contemporaneity. The Bible is paradoxically both an ancient and a very modern book. It speaks of the past, but it also speaks to the present (when it is allowed to speak), because it speaks to the basic problems that now and always have confronted human beings: Who am I? What am I? and What is my destiny?

The Bible has in the past provided an authentic word by which men and women who looked to it could find the answers to life's meaning and purpose. That is the Christian alternative today. I want to close by referring to the latent value that the Bible possesses for fulfilling the purposes of this university.

We might ponder for a moment that the humanities were the reason for the development of universities, and despite the emphasis on science in this university, the concerns of the humanities still infuse the reason for the existence of this institution, and others like it, to a remarkable degree. Have you ever wondered what the purposes of a university are? Well, a committee of distinguished faculty on this campus pondered our purpose a few years ago. They were attempting to address that question because it had been raised by the board of regents. The results of their efforts were published and were endorsed by the University Faculty Assembly on April 15, 1970. The document states that: "the primary purpose of a University is to provide an environment in which faculty and students can discover, examine critically, preserve, and transmit the knowledge, wisdom, and values that will help ensure the survival of the present and future generations with improvement in the quality of life."[11]

Other purposes are mentioned: "(1) to provide students with optimum opportunity from the heritage of the past, for gaining experience in the use of their intelligent and creative capacities, and for developing themselves as concerned, responsible, humane citizens; (2) to extend the frontiers of knowledge through research; and (3) to provide society with objective information and with imaginative approaches to the solutions of problems which can serve as a basis for sound decision-making in all areas."

You will notice in the above statement some concern for such matters as "values," "improvement in the quality of life," a concern for "learning from the heritage of the past" and for individual development "as concerned, responsible, humane citizens." The professors who worked out that statement of purpose believed that faculty and students should be future oriented and that their joint efforts would provide not only knowledge and skills but also social values because much of the leadership for the next generation comes out of the university. In fact, they said that "the University has an obligation to examine and to preserve the value judgments that can *elevate the condition of the society on which it depends.*"[12] The future-oriented search for truth should explicitly recognize the need to transmit not only knowledge but also meaningful value judgment to succeeding generations.

The committee enthusiastically quoted the words of the then Secretary of Health, Education and Welfare, John W. Gardner, who had written that

Young people do not assimilate the values of their group by learning the words (truth, justice, etc.) and their definitions. They learn these in intensely personal transactions with their immediate families or associates. They learn them in the routines and crises of living, but they also learn them through songs, stories, drama and games. They do not learn ethical principles; they emulate ethical (or unethical) people. They do not analyze or list the attributes. That is why young people need models, both in their imaginative life and in their environment, *models of what man at his best can be.* [13]

The point of all this is to state that the committee, who spoke for the faculty and the regents, had a proper interest in the humanistic concerns of values, of elevating the condition of society, of the development of individuals into concerned, responsible, humane citizens.

The secular dogma under which this institution operates is that there is no God. But there is no hope in man. The literature we read, the movies we see and national TV all assail us with proof that human beings are immoral, selfish and inherently bent on taking advantage of others.

The Christian alternative is the biblical view that there is a purpose and a power outside ourselves. Since that is true, it is possible for us to become what we have the potential to become but not the power. We can be renewed by the renewing of our minds when we cooperate with "the God who is there." Through him we can find meaning and purpose and fulfillment here and now, plus a rich destiny beyond this life. The Bible is the reliable source on which the Christian alternative is based. It speaks of the eternal Creator in whom we live and move and have our being.

Notes

[1]Madalyn Murray O'Hair, *What on Earth Is an Atheist?* The Atheist Viewpoint, vol. 2 (New York: Arno Press and The New York Times, 1972), pp. 245-46.
[2]Ibid.
[3]Ibid.
[4]Ibid., p. 249.
[5]Robert F. Bartley, *The Starstudded Hoax of Christianity with its Allied Gods* (Toledo: Robert F. Bartley, 1969), p. 21.
[6]Ibid., p. 234.
[7]F. F. Bruce, "Are the New Testament Documents Still Reliable?" *Christianity Today* (20 Oct. 1978), pp. 28-33.
[8]British Museum No. 91032. Taylor Prism.
[9]*Biblical Archaeologist* (March 1978), pp. 29ff.
[10]W. F. Albright, *History, Archaeology and Christian Humanism* (New York: McGraw Hill, 1964), p. 56.
[11]UW—Madison Faculty Document 279.
[12]Ibid. (italics mine).
[13]John W. Gardner, *Self-Renewal: The Individual and the Innovative Society* (New York: Harper and Row, 1963), p. 124 (italics mine).

Recommended Reading:

Finegan, Jack. *Light From the Ancient Past.* 2 vols. Princeton: Princeton Univ. Press, 1959.

Horn, Siegfried H. "Biblical Archaeology After 30 Years (1948-1978)." *Occasional Papers of the Horn Archaeological Museum.* Berrien Springs, Michigan: Andrews University, No. 1, 1978.

Kenyon, Kathleen M. *The Bible and Recent Archaeology.* Atlanta: John Knox Press, 1978.

Kitchen, Kenneth A. *Ancient Orient and Old Testament.* Downers Grove: InterVarsity Press, 1966.

——————— *The Bible in Its World.* Downers Grove: InterVarsity Press, 1978.

Lapp, Paul W. *Biblical Archaeology and History.* New York: World Publishing Company, 1969.

Schoville, Keith N. *Biblical Archaeology in Focus.* Grand Rapids: Baker Book House, 1978.

Yamauchi, E. *The Stones and the Scriptures.* London: Inter-Varsity Press, 1973.

Chapter 6
Christianity, Modern Medicine and the Whole Person

A. A. MacKinney

Health is a complex concept which means optimal functioning of both body and mind. Today there is a great deal of emphasis on the body. We have body-building machines, jogging programs, health foods, glamour magazines and tennis camps. We try to retain our youth and beauty at considerable cost. Let us suppose in fantasy that we could provide ourselves with the perfect body: Elizabeth Taylor's eyes, Farrah Fawcett's hair, Jimmy Carter's teeth, Arnold Schwartznegger's muscles, Albert Einstein's brain —a perfect set of equipment. Yet if we had nothing to do and life had no meaning, that perfect body would be of little use. We might give our right arm to be happy. Mental, emotional and spiritual health is probably as important as, if not more important than, physical health. It is possible to have part of the body missing or defective and yet to function extremely well.

Health is also complicated because there are two ways of arriving at health: one is prevention of disease, or

what is called preventive medicine. The other is intervention with disease, or what is called therapeutic medicine.
There is a tension in our country between the two kinds of
medicine, with the balance currently in favor of therapeutic
medicine. One-hundred-sixty billion dollars in 1976 was
spent on medical care. It is not certain how all those funds
were allocated, but of federal funds which were spent for
health in that year, 92 per cent was used for the treatment
of the sick, 5 per cent was used for environmental protec-
tion, 3 per cent was used for research and 1 per cent was
spent on problems of lifestyle.[1] Therapeutic medicine is
more powerful politically than preventive medicine because sick people have many more pressing problems than
well people. And hospitals, drug and supply houses, elec-
tronics companies and doctors make money from sick
people. It is possible to pay $50,000 or even more for being
sick; most people will not pay that to stay well.

Yet there is compelling evidence that preventive medicine is better than therapeutic medicine. It is much less
expensive, and logically it is better to stay healthy than to
try to fix the damages. In this talk I will attempt to explore
the relationship between preventive medicine and therapeutic medicine in the biblical context and in our modern
world, and to correlate those two medical models with
Christian principles.

A Christian View of Health

First let us look at the Christian perspective on health. A
Christian view of health begins with the origin of disease.
The Old Testament teaches that man and woman were
created physically perfect, highly intelligent and able to
walk with God as one walks with a friend. Man and woman
were offered, because they had free will, the option of rejecting fellowship with God. Incredibly, they aligned themselves against God, exposing themselves to pain and death
and carrying the rest of the creation into grief, illness and

futility. Consequently, sickness as we know it is due in general to humanity's rebellion against God. Sometimes, in addition, sickness is due to specific errors of individuals themselves. I will not imply that all disease is due to a person's wrongdoing but rather that much illness is due to personal errors and wrong choices and that we must learn how to prevent those kinds of illnesses.

Old Testament Medicine

Old Testament medicine is almost entirely preventive. There is essentially no direction for treatment of disease in the Old Testament (actually, one poultice was recommended) but much direction was given about prevention of disease. The Old Testament Law contained detailed rules about food, sanitation, sexual conduct and work. For example, the kinds of wild and domestic animals, birds and fish that could be eaten were specified. Sanitation rules prescribed the isolation of persons in contact with dead animals or dead people, the isolation of women after childbirth and soldiers after battle, and the disposal of wastes. The concept of quarantine comes from those sanitary laws. Rules for sexual conduct forbade adultery, homosexuality, prostitution and incest. The main rule about work was a required rest of one day in seven. All of those regulations can be shown to have merit in preventing disease or illness. But the most important regulation of all was to love God and keep his commandments, not only laws designed for the maintenance of health, but all of the laws, some of which pertained to religious ceremonies and others which specified proper treatment of neighbors, strangers and the poor. It is clear from the Old Testament record that both Israel's physical health and its national prosperity depended on obedience to God (Deut. 28:1-24). It is worth quoting at length.

And if you obey the voice of the LORD your God, being careful to do all his commandments which I command you this day, the LORD your God will set you high above all the nations of the earth. And all these blessings shall come upon you and overtake you, if you obey the voice of the LORD your God. Blessed shall you be in the city, and blessed shall you be in the field. Blessed shall be the fruit of your body, and the fruit of your ground, and the fruit of your beasts, the increase of your cattle, and the young of your flock. Blessed shall be your basket and your kneading-trough. Blessed shall you be when you come in, and blessed shall you be when you go out.

The LORD will cause your enemies who rise against you to be defeated before you; they shall come out against you one way, and flee before you seven ways. The LORD will command the blessing upon you in your barns, and in all that you undertake; and he will bless you in the land which the LORD your God gives you. The LORD will establish you as a people holy to himself, as he has sworn to you, if you keep the commandments of the LORD your God, and walk in his ways. And all the peoples of the earth shall see that you are called by the name of the LORD; and they shall be afraid of you. And the LORD will make you abound in prosperity, in the fruit of your body, and in the fruit of your cattle, and in the fruit of your ground, within the land which the LORD swore to your fathers to give you. The LORD will open to you his good treasury the heavens, to give the rain of your land in its season and to bless all the work of your hands; and you shall lend to many nations, but you shall not borrow. And the LORD will make you the head, and not the tail; and you shall tend upward only, and not downward; if you obey the commandments of the LORD your God, which I command you this day, being careful to do them, and if you do not turn aside from any of the words which I command you this day, to the right hand or to the left, to go after other gods to serve them.

But if you will not obey the voice of the LORD your God

or be careful to do all his commandments and his statutes which I command you this day, then all these curses shall come upon you and overtake you. Cursed shall you be in the city, and cursed shall you be in the field. Cursed shall be your basket and your kneading-trough. Cursed shall be the fruit of your body, and the fruit of your ground, the increase of your cattle, and the young of your flock. Cursed shall you be when you come in, and cursed shall you be when you go out.

The LORD will send upon you curses, confusion, and frustration, in all that you undertake to do, until you are destroyed and perish quickly, on account of the evil of your doings, because you have forsaken me. The LORD will make the pestilence cleave to you until he has consumed you off the land which you are entering to take possession of it. The LORD will smite you with consumption, and with fever, inflammation, and fiery heat, and with drought, and with blasting, and with mildew; they shall pursue you until you perish. And the heavens over your head shall be brass, and the earth under you shall be iron. The LORD will make the rain of your land powder and dust; from heaven it shall come down upon you until you are destroyed.

New Testament Medicine

When we turn to the New Testament, we find confirmation of Old Testament preventive-medicine teachings, but the therapeutic model is definitely in the foreground. Perhaps that is an implicit criticism of Israel's failure to obey the Law. Jesus healed people with all kinds of disease: epilepsy, blindness, deafness, atrophy of the arm, intractable menstrual bleeding, edema, paralysis and leprosy. On three occasions he raised dead people to life. The healings were in many instances accompanied by faith in Christ. Faith-healing in Christ's day was different from the popular understanding of that phenomenon today. Faith-healing was a reaching out to Christ for a power that he possessed. It was not based on some inward power of the sick person. Healing was accompanied by a faith in Christ so that a change in the person's lifestyle accompanied the healing. Faith was reconciliation with God and was not "faith in faith."

Jesus' acts of healing proclaimed the kingdom of God as an invasion of the world and demonstrated his credentials as the Son of God. None of Jesus' disciples had the degree of healing power that he exhibited. He was uniquely the great physician.

Any fair evaluation of the record shows that Jesus' healings were not hypnotic or psychosomatic. One cannot consider congenital blindness psychosomatic. One cannot heal leprosy by hypnosis. One cannot raise a child from the dead by the power of suggestion.

One might inquire why Jesus' disciples could heal then, when they cannot heal now. It is not entirely correct to say that they cannot heal now. Some people are healed without adequate explanation today. And Christians affirm that all healing, like all life, is from God. Although there is a new interest in faith-healing, we do not see anything like the success of the first-century Christians. Many biblical scholars believe that, from the biblical record, miracles may not be expected on any continuing basis. "Miraculous events" related to health and healing are clustered around three periods in history: the time of the exodus of Israel from Egypt around 1450 B.C.; the period around 850 B.C. when Elijah and Elisha were prophets in Israel; and during and shortly after the life of Christ. All three periods were times of spiritual crisis.

A most important aspect of Jesus' healing ministry in addition to his gifts of physical healing was the work of emotional and spiritual healing. We see that in Matthew 6:25-34 as well as throughout the Gospels.

Therefore I tell you, do not be anxious about your life, what you shall eat or what you shall drink, nor about your body, what you shall put on. Is not life more than food, and the body more than clothing? Look at the birds of the air: they neither sow nor reap nor gather into barns, and yet your heavenly Father feeds them. Are you not of more value than they? And which of you by being anxious can add one cubit to his span of life? And why are you anxious about clothing? Consider the lilies of the field, how they grow; they neither toil nor spin; yet I tell you, even Solomon in all his glory was not arrayed like one of these. But if God so clothes the grass of the field, which today is alive and tomorrow is thrown into the oven, will he not much more clothe you, O men of little faith? Therefore do not be anxious, saying, "What shall we eat?" or "What shall we drink?" or "What shall we wear?" For the Gentiles seek all these things; and your heavenly Father knows that you need them all. But seek first his kingdom and his righteousness, and all these things shall be yours as well.

Therefore do not be anxious about tomorrow, for tomorrow will be anxious for itself. Let the day's own trouble be sufficient for the day.

But Jesus did not merely talk about anxiety, he accomplished an action that revolutionizes our concept of death and our anxiety about death. In Jesus' death and resurrection we find the proof of life after death which he demonstrated in himself and promised to those who have faith in him. The demonstration of life after death and the promise of his continuing fellowship have the potential to relieve the greatest fear of modern men and women, the fear of nonbeing. At the center of anxiety is the fear of death, and the core of that fear is the fear of nonbeing. As the writer of Hebrews says, he came to "deliver those who through fear of death were subject to lifelong bondage" (2:14-15).

Medicine: Middle Ages to the Present
In the centuries after the death of Christ, the truth of

Christ's life and work and the lessons of Old Testament hygiene became confused. Preventive medicine disappeared. The Middle Ages endured widespread plagues. Treatments by physicians were sometimes ridiculous. A treatment for epilepsy was compounded of acid mixed with lime until it turned yellow then saturated with alcohol to which mistletoe, hearts of peonies, elk hoofs and a pulverized skull of an executed malefactor were added. Those ingredients were distilled to dryness, mixed with castor oil, elephant's lice, salt of peony, alcohol, oil of anise and so on. Surely such a medicine would give a person a seizure who had never had one before!

With the Renaissance, Reformation and rebirth of knowledge, simple observations led the way to the modern era of public health. Preventive medicine again became dominant. For example, in 1853 there was a severe outbreak of cholera in London. John Snow mapped the prevalence of cholera in various parts of London and found an eightfold greater infection rate in homes served by one water company compared with another. He reported that nature had devised an experiment "on the grandest scale in that no fewer than 500,000 people of both sexes, of every age and occupation, and of every rank and station from gentle folks down to the very poor were divided into two groups without their choice and in most cases without their knowledge, one group being supplied with water containing the sewage of London and amongst it whatever might have come from the cholera patients, the other group having water quite free from such impurities. To turn this grand experiment to account, all that was required was to learn the supply of water to each individual house where a fatal attack of cholera might occur." John Snow knew little bacteriology, but the history of medicine suggests that the plagues were controlled before either bacteriology developed as a science or antibiotic use came into existence.

A hundred years ago, William Osler listed the plagues that were coming under control during the nineteenth century: anthrax, leprosy, tuberculosis, typhoid, diphtheria, cholera, lockjaw, bubonic plague, yellow fever, smallpox, typhus, rabies, malaria. Those scourges that cost millions of lives are practically unknown to college students today, largely because of the successful application of preventive medicine. At the time those diseases came under control, treatment for them was not available. For example, death from tuberculosis began to decline in 1850, a hundred years before isoniazid and other antituberculous drugs were known. Mortality from scarlet fever, measles and whooping cough was also declining years before modern immunizations and antibiotics were available.

Control of infection has occurred because of simple measures such as isolation of infected persons, clean water, improved housing and nutrition. And we must mention soap and water to wash clothes and wash bodies. When Thomas a Becket was murdered in the Canterbury cathedral in 1170, the vermin crawling out of his clothing had the onlookers bursting out laughing amid their weeping. Six hundred years later, in 1746, George Washington wrote, "Kill no vermin as fleas, lice, ticks, etc., in the sight of others." Describing the education of a French princess in the seventeenth century, a court advisor said, "One had carefully taught the young princess that it was bad manners to scratch when one did it by habit and not by necessity and it was improper to take lice or fleas or other vermin by the neck to kill them in company except in the most intimate circles." A writer in 1804, describing the hot summers on the eastern seaboard, spoke of the vast numbers of Americans who passed through a long life "amidst all these heats, clothed in cloth, flannel, and black fur hats and lying on a featherbed at night drinking nothing but wine and port and eating strong meats three times a day and never allowing water to touch any part of them but their extremities for a year together."

But gradually people learned about the bath. On July 31, 1798, a prominent Philadelphia woman named Mrs. Drinker wrote in her diary, "Nancy pulled a string of the showerbath again this evening. She seems better reconciled to it. The water has stood some hours in the yard which alters the property some [i.e., makes it warmer] and she goes under the bath in a single gown and an oilcloth cap." The following year, Mrs. Drinker herself finally took a bath: "Nancy came here this evening. She and self went into the showerbath. I bore it better than I expected not having been wet all over at once for 28 years past."[2]

Thanks to clean water and, recently, somewhat cleaner air, personal hygiene, good diet, immunization, isolation from infectious agents, sewage and garbage disposal, we enjoy a longer, healthier life than any people in history. The preventive medicine model has been very effective. Smallpox may have been eradicated in the late 1970s.

Diseases of Lifestyle

But preventive medicine has exposed a new set of diseases that are called the diseases of lifestyle. In some hospitals, two-thirds of the patients can be found suffering from diseases of lifestyle. The diseases of lifestyle are all preventable, but they are the result of habits too pleasurable or too difficult to break. All will agree that clean water, good food, pleasant-smelling streets and good housing are desirable. Not all agree that abstinence from alcohol, tobacco, drugs, promiscuous indulgence in sex, overeating and driving fast vehicles are desirable. Abuse of alcohol has led to significant disability in 5 per cent of Americans, and in some subsets of the population 50 per cent of the people are partially or seriously disabled by alcohol. Misuse of alcohol leads to brain damage, ruined livers, broken marriages and premature death. Newspaper reports suggest that in 50 per cent of automobile accidents and 30 per cent of snowmobile accidents alcohol is a factor. People who smoke cigarettes have a death rate 70-120 per cent higher than control groups. Tobacco smoking leads to destroyed lungs and cancer of lip, tongue, larynx, lung and perhaps pancreas. Misuse of food leads to diabetes, shortened life span and a significant risk for surgery and accidents. Misuse of sex is reported to lead to sterility for 50,000 American women a year. Gonorrhea is completely out of control in this country. Syphilis is not under control. The "sexual revolution" has added to the original five venereal diseases at least ten others. Although newspaper reports pay a great deal of attention to airplane disasters, the number of people who die on the highways as a result of automobile accidents generates little concern. More Americans were killed by automobiles during the period of the Vietnam war than died in combat. And all of these diseases of lifestyle are preventable—but physicians are helpless to help people who will not and cannot stop doing the things that are killing them. Consequently, therapeutic medicine is again in the foreground.

Man: Machine or Whole Person
As therapeutic medicine reasserts itself, it fosters a dissociation between the person and the illness. The patient is frequently treated like a mechanical device such as an automobile that needs a fender straightened, a carburetor adjusted, a new set of windshield wipers or some higher octane gasoline. The sick person usually encourages that approach. One woman who came to the emergency room repeatedly with razor slashes on her face and body said: "I got my way of living and you got yours. Just sew me up and let me go." The fact that there is a "driver" in the human "machine" is usually ignored, yet frequently it is the "driver" rather than his or her "machine" that is at fault. It seems to me to be pointless to keep unbending the fenders when plainly the driver is unwilling or unable to steer properly.

How are people to prevent the diseases of lifestyle? Secular humanism has one suggestion: people need education. The Christian challenges secular humanism by asserting that people are not fully able to respond to education. They are slaves to passions and need to be liberated by the Spirit of God. The two hypotheses can be tested on a population of well-educated people—physicians and nurses in the United States. If the humanist's optimistic view of man is correct, we should find that all physicians and nurses abstain from alcohol, tobacco, drugs, overindulgence in food and promiscuous sex and the use of fast vehicles. The data are to the contrary. There is a higher incidence of alcoholism and drug abuse among physicians than in the normal population. Most physicians have given up smoking but most nurses have picked up where the physicians left off. And one could go on to mention the other diseases as well.

A professor of psychiatry once said that it was an article of faith with him that if you tell people what is right they will do it. A brash sophomore in the back row piped up and said, "If that were true, no doctors would smoke cigarettes." The truth is that people live by what they love, not by what they know.

But even if telling people what is right were acceptable, some would disagree about what is correct advice. Is it right to tell a patient to stop drinking because he has cirrhosis? My colleagues say yes. Is it right to tell a patient to stop being promiscuous because he has gonorrhea? My colleagues say no.

The healing of the person (in contrast to healing the disease) is outside the reach of the current medical model. Pills may allay your anxiety. Psychiatry can give you a better opinion of yourself. Physical therapy may restore your ability to work. But medicine cannot give you a reason for your existence, purge away your guilt, remove your existential dread of death or turn you away from destructive habits.

In response to this defect in the medical model, we now have a bewildering array of quasi-medical attempts to deal with the whole person. They include hypnosis, acupuncture, mind-control, meditation, rolfing, bio-feedback and scientology, mixed with Taoism, Sufism and other sorts of mystical religions. The latest word is that medicine and religion are going to have a love affair. Beyond secular humanism, I see medicine threatened by all sorts of loose-thinking psychics, Shamans, spiritualists and mystics pushing what is called holistic medicine. Their assumption is that you are a part of God and that, by mobilizing the spiritual power within you, you can get well and stay well.

The assumption that we are a part of God is incorrect. God is completely different and separate from us. We are normally alienated from him. We come into our best state of spiritual and mental health when we are reconciled to him and then his Spirit indwells us. He has laid out the conditions for our reconciliation in great detail. We are reconciled to God only through the death of his Son.

Notes
[1]Anne Sommers, letter to the editor, *New England Journal of Medicine* (1978), p. 746.
[2]The quotations from George Washington and other figures from history are taken from Harold D. Eberlein, "When Society First Took a Bath," *Sickness and Health in America,* eds. J. W. Leavitt and R. L. Numbers (Madison: Univ. of Wisconsin Press, 1978), pp. 331-41.

Recommended Reading

Allen, David E., Lewis P. Bird and Robert Herrmann, eds. *Whole-Person Medicine.* Downers Grove: InterVarsity Press, 1980.

"Holistic Health Issue," *Spiritual Counterfeits Project Journal,* August 1978 (P. O. Box 2418, Berkeley, CA 94702).

Leavitt, J. W. and R. L. Numbers, eds. *Sickness and Health in America.* Madison: Univ. of Wisconsin Press, 1978.

Tournier, Paul. *Guilt and Grace.* New York: Harper and Row, 1962.

Chapter 7
And Then . . .

Peter Wilkes

In the preceding pages five scholars have argued the intellectual case for Christianity. In a university setting that is all one might expect. Universities are, after all, cerebral places. Such a purely intellectual approach, however, does scant justice to the wholeness of Christianity.

It has been the speakers' contention that the secular outlook offers an inadequate approach to human nature. Yet its inadequacy is most clearly demonstrated not in the lecture room but in life itself.

At the end of the day, scientists, economists, physicians and archaeologists go home to assume roles as parents and husbands or wives. It is in such practical areas of relationships where the alienation that is the logical consequence of secular humanism most often reveals itself. The breakdown may seem particularly poignant when a person is undeniably competent in some professional or intellectual realm.

The most important reason to consider becoming a Christian is *a conscious need for a fresh beginning, an awareness of inadequacy in oneself.* In intellectual argument the problem is presented as if it were outside me. In fact, I *am* the problem in microcosm.

Jesus, in calling men and women to follow him, intended a transformation of the whole person. The preaching of the apostles also was based on a radical change experienced in becoming a Christian. When Peter announced to a crowd in the temple, "Repent therefore, and turn again" (Acts 3:19), he was presenting the real issue for those who wished to become Christians.

All of us who have lectured in this series want to make it clear that to be intellectually convinced or attracted to the case we have presented is *not* the same thing as becoming a Christian. It is only a first step. This final chapter is concerned with the remaining steps.

At some point in our lives most of us feel inadequate. Those feelings are pointers to a much deeper insight, one that is difficult for most people to face: the inadequacy in us lies in our relationship with God. In that relationship the key issue is a moral one. We are simply not good enough, none of us.

From the very beginning the Judeo-Christian experience of God has been that he is morally pure to a degree beyond our imagining. He is not merely good; he is goodness itself. Facing such purity, human beings always become conscious of personal impurity. "Depart from me, for I am a sinful man, O Lord" (Lk. 5:8).

It is of course entirely right for us to feel that way, because we have been made by God. Our existence is dependent on his choice. And he wants us to be good, not by our warped standards but by his. That is not merely an arbitrary demand placed on our lives. Our world is locked in an ultimate moral struggle between good and evil. The battle, which clearly rages outside in the world, also rages internally in all of us. Making a moral choice means taking sides. Either we are committed to God and to goodness, love and life, or we are opposed to those values and to their source.

In that ultimate conflict there are no private, independent forces. We cannot strike out on our own. To try to do so is to exhibit exactly the spirit of pride that wars against goodness.

The horrifying feature in this conflict is that *we are already on the wrong side.* That is why the purity and goodness of God are so intimidating to us and invoke such guilt.

Jesus is the ultimate revelation of the conflict. He stands alone at the end, relentlessly forcing human beings to choose. And choose they do. Roman justice is prostituted to political survival by Pilate. Jewish religious law is suborned by a high priest and his colleagues. A crowd is bribed to cry for his blood. His disciples flee and Peter denies ever knowing him. The world is there in microcosm, and where the world's heart lies is clear for all to see.

To become a Christian, of course, one must acknowledge where one stands in the conflict and give up any attempt to avoid responsibility. Wisdom begins when I, like the prodigal son in the Bible, go home and say, "Father, I have sinned against heaven and before you" (Lk. 15:18). To admit our rebellious nature is hard for us but absolutely essential for reconciliation with our heavenly Father.

God's response to a genuine turning away from our rebellion is dramatic. Relief from our burden of moral guilt is immediate. The problem has been placed in the Father's hands, and his action is decisive. Sin and guilt are simply annihilated and our forgiveness is proclaimed. The emphatic language of Scripture underscores the point: "As far as the east is from the west, so far does he remove our transgressions from us" (Ps. 103:12).

Such forgiveness is incredibly costly, not to us but to God. The cross of Jesus is more than a display of human sinfulness; it is also a triumph of God's grace. There, as our representative, God himself bears all the consequences of our human rebellion against his goodness. Our rejection of him has been a rejection of life as well as of goodness; in the end they are the same. The consequence of our rejection is therefore death. It is *our* death Jesus bears for us.

Yet the last word is with life, for, like goodness, in God's universe life is invincible. The second triumph of Jesus was his return from death. Just as commitment of ourselves (and our rebellion) into his hands leads to forgiveness by his death, so his victory over death leads to an experience of life in us. We are not only forgiven, we are reborn.

Hence the second step in entering the Christian life is commitment to being changed under his hand into a new and better person. The conflict has changed from a rebellion to a struggle against evil in my own life. This is not a kind of self-reformation, which would be a return to the old pattern of self-justification, of trying to impress God with my accomplishments. It is different now: *he* is actively changing me. The decisive power in molding my character over the years of my life is his. To be a Christian is to commit myself to being transformed, on a continuing basis, toward a quality of goodness that is all his. The Bible speaks of this as being conformed to the likeness of Jesus (Rom. 8:29).

It is at times a painful process. We do not lightly let go of our pride or our prejudice or our cherished self-images. But it is a sure process. God does not begin tasks and leave them unfinished. We have the guarantee that "he who began a good work in you will bring it to completion at the day of Jesus Christ" (Phil. 1:6).

There will be a day when, as his completed workmanship, we will stand before him. On that day we shall no longer be ashamed, nor shall we be guilty. We shall be fully transformed into his goodness and his life.

We shall be our Father's children, grown up at last.

If you have come with us this far from the heavily intellectual start of this book, you may be ready for one further
thought. The ultimate attraction to Christian faith is not
in our needs or our guilt; it lies in Jesus himself.

In the end, Christianity comes down to loving him. We
urge you to pick up the Gospel of John and read the story
of Jesus again. You may find him so gloriously attractive
that to follow him, to be his, will be your response, too—
as it has been ours.

Contributors

Wayne M. Becker (B.S., M.S., Ph.D., University of Wisconsin-Madison) is professor of botany at the University of Wisconsin-Madison. He has done postdoctoral cancer research in Glasgow, Scotland, and sabbatical research in plant molecular biology in Edinburgh, Scotland. He has also been the guest of the Polish Academy of Sciences in Warsaw. His publications include *Energy and the Living Cell* (Philadelphia: Lippincott, 1977).

Archie A. MacKinney, Jr. (B.A., Wheaton College, Illinois; M.D., University of Rochester School of Medicine) is a hematologist and professor of medicine at the University of Wisconsin Medical School. His publications include many scientific articles in experimental biology.

J. David Richardson (B.A., McGill University; Ph.D., University of Michigan) is professor of economics at the University of Wisconsin-Madison. He is the author of *Understanding International Economics: Theory and Practice* (Boston: Little, Brown, 1980) and co-editor with Robert E. Baldwin of *International Trade and Finance: Readings* (Boston: Little, Brown, 1974). He is also chairman of the committee producing the Graduate Record Examination in economics and a research associate of the National Bureau of Economic Research.

Keith Schoville (B.A., Milligan College; M.A., Ph.D., University of Wisconsin-Madison) is chairman of the department of Hebrew and Semitic studies, University of Wisconsin-Madison. He is the author of many scholarly articles as well as the book *Biblical Archaeology in Focus* (Grand Rapids: Baker Book House, 1978).

Peter Wilkes (M.S., Ph.D., University of Manchester, England) was at the time of the lecture series professor of nuclear and metallurgical engineering at the University of Wisconsin-Madison. In addition to numerous scholarly articles, he is the author of *Solid State Theory in Metallurgy* (London: Cambridge University Press, 1973) and co-author with R. B. Nicholson and G. W. Lorimer of *The Proceedings of the International Conference on Phase Transformations* (London: Institute of Metals, 1967). He is currently associate pastor of Elmbrook Church, Waukesha, Wisconsin.